SCRAPBOOKING
WITH
MEMORY MAKERS®

Michele Gerbrandt and Kerry Arquette

BEAUX ARTS EDITIONS

IN ASSOCIATION WITH F&W PUBLICATIONS, INC.

© 1999 Hugh Lauter Levin Associates, Inc.

Project Director: Leslie C. Carola
Design: Kathleen Herlihy-Paoli, Inkstone Design
Editors: Deborah Cannarella and Leslie C. Carola
Copy Editor: Deborah T. Zindell

Photography by Jim Cambon and Carol Conway
Photo Art Direction by Ron Gerbrandt, Diane Gibbs, and Chris Ledford
Page ideas from the readers and artists of
Memory Makers® magazine, published by:
Satellite Press
475 West 115th Avenue #6
Denver, Colorado 80234

This book is co-published by Satellite Press and
Hugh Lauter Levin Associates, Inc.

Printed in Hong Kong

ISBN: 0-88363-932-7

THIS BOOK IS DEDICATED TO THE READERS OF
MEMORY MAKERS® MAGAZINE
WHO HAVE SHARED THEIR PERSONAL PAGE IDEAS,
STORIES, AND TALENTS WITH US OVER THE YEARS.

YOU ARE THE HEART OF THIS PROJECT.

CONTENTS

SCRAPBOOKING

WITH

MEMORY MAKERS®

Alexandra's 1st Laugh...

Mother's Love

PRESERVING MEMORIES

A scrapbook is magic. It captures and cradles life's most precious moments—an infant's first toothless smile, the excitement of Christmas morning, the reverence of a wedding, the fun of family get-togethers—as well as honors our lives and the lives of those we love. Through photographs, memorabilia, special thoughts, and stories, scrapbooks evoke our fondest memories and allow us to relive once-in-a-lifetime experiences.

Scrapbookers know the value of preserving memories. With scissors, paper, and imagination, they carefully create albums to revisit the special times of their lives again and again. The works of art that they create also provide inspiration for other enthusiasts.

Like painters, scrapbook artists begin with a blank page. Onto that empty canvas, they lay their photos, memorabilia, stories, and hearts. When it's complete, their album is a one-of-a-kind reflection of themselves, their lives, and those friends and family members who have shared it. A memory scrapbook is a treasured heirloom to hand down to generations to come.

◁ *MOTHER'S LOVE. Artist: Jenny Clark Friedman.*
A yellowed envelope of black-and-white baby photographs fell surreptitiously to the floor and brought with it for this artist a reconnection to the past and visual memories of a family lost in a devastating accident years before. This straightforward scrapbook page, framed by elegant die-cut vines, presents simple photographs of a baby basking in the warmth of a radiant mother's arms.

▷ *SISTERS. Artist: Pam Klassen.*
Illuminated letters are an easy and elegant way to embellish any scrapbook page or cover. Today's materials make this medieval art form accessible to crafters of all levels.

HOW IT ALL BEGAN

～～～

*I*n 1826, after more than twenty-five years of experimenting, Joseph Nicephore Niepce finally did it! He recorded the view from his workroom window—a pigeon house, a pear tree, a slanting roof of a barn—on a sheet of metal. Niepce had created the world's first permanent photograph.

Once the elusive combination of metal, light, and chemicals was discovered, other inventors refined the techniques and tools needed for picture-taking. By 1839, the first camera was available to the public, and entrepreneurs around the world opened portrait studios. By the mid-nineteenth century, many people could afford to have their pictures taken. A process was developed to make multiple prints from a single plate, and people soon began buying duplicate photographs to give away to friends and family members.

In 1860, a book containing photos of Queen Victoria, the Prince Consort, and their children became a huge commercial success, and the public began to organize their own family photos in copycat volumes. The books also included pictures of celebrities, calling cards bearing photographs of friends, passports, and other memorabilia. So began the family tradition of creating scrapbooks!

GETTING STARTED

~

There are as many types of scrapbook albums as there are stories to be told! Baby albums, heritage albums, family albums, sports albums, and school albums; anniversary, autobiography, career, and gift albums; wedding, pet, and journal albums, too. Choosing the right theme for your album can be as difficult as choosing a dessert from a buffet table laden with your favorite custards, cakes, and pies. The right choice is the one that catches your interest and fits your taste at the time. And, of course, the right theme will also depend on the types of photos and memorabilia you have collected.

CHOOSING A THEME

~

Like the people who make them, theme scrapbooks have distinct personalities. Their individuality is expressed through the artist's choice of photos, memorabilia, words, color, layout, and design. Baby albums reflect motherly love. Tribute albums honor the special qualities of their subjects. Wedding albums reflect the couples' dreams and promises. Each album tells a story that is as unique as the individual or event showcased and the artist who created the book. Memory album themes are only as limited as a scrapbooker's imagination.

◁ *RIBBONS AND LACE. Artist: Tonya Jeppson.*
A series of three distinct border treatments draws the eye to the family portraits contained within. Draw the borders with wavy rulers and a straight-edged ruler, adding color to complement.

▷ *SAN FRANCISCO. Artists: (top) Kate Young, (bottom) Jauneta Gungl.*
Place fashions memories into a mosaic of myriad colors and textures. Bits of colored paper and souvenir scrap memorabilia capture the essence of a sense of place and give personal photos wonderful context.

△ IT'S A BOY! *Artist: Julie Staub.*
Traditional hospital memorabilia incorporated with photos taken just after the baby's birth decorate a page that captures those tender moments.

▷ LADYBUGS. *Photographer: Debbie Schubert.*
A single picture tells a complete story. Children reveled in the millions of ladybugs at an Arizona campsite, pronouncing them "nice, not yucky!"

SPECIFIC THEMES: Some themes, such as weddings, vacations, family histories, and school years, are better displayed in a finite scrapbook. Like good novels, finite scrapbooks have a beginning, middle, and end. They tell the story of a specific event, set of events, or experience. Specific theme albums can be planned, organized, and designed with the entire finished project in mind. Think of the book as one continuous read, from the beginning to the end. To prevent a choppy, unplanned look, establish a consistent color scheme and style. The repeated use of a particular design element, sticker theme, or special technique will give the book a sense of unity.

ONGOING THEMES: Some theme albums are ongoing or open-ended projects. Life albums or hobby albums, for example, record activities and events that unfold over time. Children grow up, adults grow older, and new photos and pages are added to the book. The changes and the years are recorded as you turn the pages.

GETTING ORGANIZED

~

The prospect of beginning can seem almost too daunting to face: hauling those heavy boxes of saved photos, cards, and other memorabilia out of closets, dragging them down attic stairs (or worse yet, up basement steps!), and then confronting the evidence of years' worth of neglect. You peer inside a box and randomly pluck a photo from the mound. No matter how hard you try, you can't quite remember what was going on in that photograph or why you took it all those years ago. Finally, in disgust, you toss the photo back in the box and consider putting the box right back where you found it. But, stop! Storing the boxes isn't the answer. Plowing ahead is.

Once you begin organizing the photos, you'll find that the work goes quickly and isn't nearly as frustrating as you feared. Here are some steps that might help:

1. Move the boxes of photos to a well-lit area with a large work surface.

2. Decide on some categories into which you'll sort the photos. For example, you might separate them by year, activity, theme, or family member.

3. Write the category names on sticky notes. Apply the notes to different areas of your work surface, adding or deleting categories as needed.

4. Begin sorting photos. As you work, jot down any memories that the pictures inspire. Use a sticky note and attach it to the back of the photo. Add dates, too, if you remember them. (If you prefer to write dates on the backs of the photos, be sure to use photo-safe graphite pencils.)

5. When you've finished the preliminary sorting, re-sort each pile according to events, patterns, or chronological order.

6. Store each sorted pile in a safe environment, such as an acid-free photo box.

7. Throw out or re-store duplicate, damaged, or inferior photos.

STORING PHOTOS AND NEGATIVES

~~~

Store photos and negatives in acid-free and lignin-free photo-storage boxes. Some boxes are sold with extra photo-safe envelopes, which make it easy to store grouped photos together. Store negatives in negative sleeves or acid-free envelopes. Place the boxes in a cool, dark location.

It is best to store negatives and photos separately. If the photos are somehow damaged, you can use the negatives, which you have stored safely elsewhere, to make additional prints.

Organize your photos, negatives, and memorabilia, storing them in photo-safe boxes and binders. Then it's easier to decide what kind of album to make.

FINDING THE TIME

~~~

We rush to work, rush to the grocery store, rush to exercise class, and rush, rush, rush to children's dance classes, soccer games, and piano lessons. In this hurry-up world, it's challenging to find time for the hobbies that make our lives fuller and happier. But assembling albums amidst chaos is possible. All it takes is organization, creativity, and a heaping helping of commitment. Here's how some dedicated scrapbookers do it:

"I work full-time and am the mother of two children, but I find time for my favorite hobby in two ways. First, I leave my supplies out on the dining room table so that I can work at any time. Second, whenever I take a long car trip, I take along my scrapbooking suppplies, and a bag for my cropping crumbs. Then I get someone else to drive!" —Mitzi Adkinson, Albany, Georgia

"As the mother of small children, the time I have to work on scrapbook pages often comes in five- or ten-minute snatches, which is enough provided my materials are close at hand. I cleared out my dining room buffet drawers and filled them with my supplies. (I work on my albums more often than I entertain!)"
—Laurie Bratten, Highlands Ranch, Colorado

"My five-year-old doesn't bother my supplies because I set up a child's desk next to my table and stocked it with paper, markers, crayons, glue, and coloring books. When I sit down to work on my albums, my daughter joins me at her desk."
—Marsha Peacock, Jacksonville, Florida

"My suggestion to those who find it too distracting to scrapbook at home is to sign up for workshops. They are a great place to make new friends and get fresh ideas as well as complete pages with no interruptions."
—Suzanne Feinberg, Palos Verdes Estates, California

TIPS FOR KEEPING ON TRACK

* *Keep supplies handy.*
* *Set aside time each month to work on albums.*
* *Schedule cropping parties with friends.*
* *Sign up for scrapbook workshops.*
* *Take supplies along on car, train, or plane trips.*
* *Take supplies along on vacations.*
* *Srapbook while waiting for kids who are in lessons or sports practice.*
* *Scrapbook instead of reading before turning in some nights.*
* *Scrapbook one hour for each hour you spend watching TV.*
* *Scrapbook for one hour each time you pick up a developed roll of film.*
* *Throw seasonal scrapbooking parties.*
* *Hold family scrapbooking nights.*

CROPPING PARTIES

Quilting bees are as traditional as apple pie. Throughout our country's history, women have put aside the chores and picked up their fabric and needles. They meet to stitch, share, talk, support, and enjoy each other. The joy of the quilting bee lives on! Today, women are reaching for their albums, paper, photos, and tools, and gathering for cropping parties—the modern-day version of the traditional bees! These women are as passionate about their scrapbooks as their ancestors were about fabrics. Like each quilt square, each scrapbook page is lovingly made, and each tells a story. While they are enjoying conversation and companionship, they also:

* Learn new scrapbooking techniques
* Share scrapbooking ideas
* Encourage and support each other's creativity
* Share tools, such as punches and scissors
* Trade stickers and paper and other supplies

The most important things to bring to a cropping party—other than plenty of photos, of course—are your enthusiasm and imagination. Then it's sure to be a success. A cropping party may be as casual an occasion as an afternoon activity at a neighbor's while the two of you are waiting for the school bus to drop off your children, or as large an event as convention-sized gatherings of hundreds of scrapbooking enthusiasts who come together for day-long workshops.

Regularly scheduled cropping parties help scrapbookers devote uninterrupted time to their hobby. Just invite some of your scrapbooking friends over for a bit of food and drink (always with lids or caps—a spill can ruin the night). Add some door prizes (stickers, punches, and maybe some fancy papers). Invite an "expert" guest who can demonstrate some new techniques. Be sure there's plenty of time to admire each other's work, and you've got all the ingredients you need for an evening of memory-making fun!

Cropping parties are held on a regular basis across the country. It is at these events that scrapbookers share their stories, tips, and techniques, just as quilters have for many generations. As many as two thousand avid scrapbookers participate in events such as this one in Denver, Colorado, to celebrate the art and craft of preserving family history.

Childhood
Christmas Memories
are the quilt pieces
of our family
history!

1967 · 1968 · 1969 · 1970 · 1966 · 1971 · 1972 · 1973

QUILT. Artist: Patricia Bissinger.
A collage of color, texture, and pattern, this picture quilt of Christmas memories is pieced with red and green square
and octagonal shapes cut from 8 1/2 x 11-inch sheets of acid-free paper. The strong, solid colors provide effective
mats for the photographs.

THE RIGHT ALBUM

~~~

It's all in the book—the scrapbook, that is. Choosing the right album is exciting, but can also be confusing and intimidating. The scrapbook album aisle at your local hobby or scrapbooking store offers such a variety! What should you look for?

THE RIGHT MATERIALS

~~~

In days gone by, photographs were stacked and adhered to album pages with schoolroom paste. There the photos stayed until the adhesive gave way, and the pictures fluttered out of the books and onto floors. Those crude methods were abandoned when magnetic albums were developed, allowing scrapbook makers to sandwich photos between self-adhesive pages and layers of plastic.

Magnetic albums are still popular because of their convenience, but many people claim that the sticky pages make it difficult to move or remove the photos. They also worry about damaging their photos and memorabilia.

An increasing awareness of the ways that chemicals interact and damage photos and memorabilia has made album enthusiasts cautious about the papers, adhesives, and inks they use in their albums. Safe products may cost more than others, but the investment in high-quality scrapbooking supplies protects the investment you've already made in film, processing, time, and priceless memories. But now there is a large selection of photo-safe albums and materials.

Savvy scrapbookers look for words such as "acid-free" and "lignin-free" when shopping for album and paper products. These materials will not damage photos, memorabilia, or scrapbook pages.

ACID-FREE: Although many paper products are touted as acid-free, look for products with pH levels in the 7 to 8.5 range. Papers that are more acidic (above 8.5) become brittle, crumble, and turn to dust over time. The photos they contact can fade or become discolored.

◁ *A PLACE IN HISTORY. Artist: Anita Hickinbotham.*
Our stories are best told in the reminiscing voice of individuals. History gives us a sense of time and place, but it is the individual's voice that gives us the sense of ourselves. We can relate to the world at large when we understand our place within it. "When you realize that an ancestor was exactly your age when a big world event happened, you understand more clearly how she felt and thought in response," says the artist.

Although convenient, scrapbookers have been discouraged by the condition with which magnetic albums have left their photographs over the years.

LIGNIN-FREE: Lignin, a substance produced within the cells of plants to strengthen the plant fibers, is naturally present in paper. It is believed that when exposed to ultraviolet light, paper that has not had the lignin removed will turn yellow.

BUFFERED: Even true acid-free papers may become acidic over time as they react to the chemicals used in their manufacture and the acids with which they come in contact. In order to protect against acidic changes, paper must be treated with an alkaline substance. This buffering process will prevent the paper from becoming acidic and absorbing the acid from memorabilia you may include in your album.

PAGE PROTECTORS: These plastic sleeves, made in a variety of sizes, are designed to fit over album pages. They protect the pages from fingerprints, grease, dust, spills, smudges, and abrasion. They also separate and protect photos from any nonarchival-quality (acidic) papers and products on the facing page. Only buy protectors that do not contain polyvinyl chloride (PVC). This chemical emits gases, causing photos to discolor and fade.

THE RIGHT SIZE

Before you even leave home, assemble the photos and memorabilia that will be included in your scrapbook. The quantity and the physical size and shape of your materials will determine the size of the album you need. Large and numerous items, such as newspaper clippings, greeting cards, and portraits, require a large album—a 12-inch by 12-inch book, for example. If your photos and memorabilia are smaller and fewer—or if you think you might be intimidated by a large, blank page—consider purchasing an album that is 8 inches by 10 inches or 8 1/2 inches by 11 inches.

THE RIGHT STYLE

~~~

*A*n average album price can range from about $10 to $50, with covers of fabric, leather, or paper. Take your time when choosing your album. You'll be living with your scrapbook for many years, so be sure to buy one that you'll continue to enjoy and that will hold up even after hundreds of viewings.

Here are a few of the standard styles you can choose from:

THREE-RING BINDERS: Similar to our old school notebooks, these albums contain plastic page protectors or top loaders that are mounted on binder rings. The scrapbook pages slide in and out of the openings at the tops of the protectors. With this particular style of binder, you can use different-colored papers for the pages throughout your album. Be sure the binders you use are made

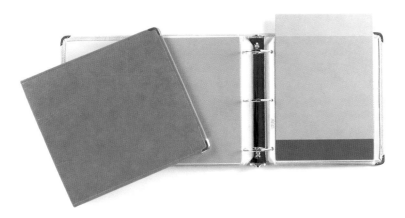

Three-ring binder albums

Spiral-bound albums

Strap-style albums

Post-bound albums

SCRAPBOOKER'S TIPS

....

—from Diane Greenlaw, Highlands Ranch, Colorado

PUTTING ON PAGE PROTECTORS

Page protectors often catch on photos and memorabilia as they are pulled over the album page of post-bound, strap-style, or spiral-bound albums. In order to prevent catching and dislodging materials, cut a sheet of wax paper slightly more than twice the width of the page. Wrap the wax paper loosely around the album page. Then pull the page protector over the wrapped album page. Once the protector is in place, slip the wax paper free.

with photo-safe materials. Vinyl, for instance, is not considered a photo-safe material but an acid-free cloth is. The page protectors should be made of PVC-free plastic.

SPIRAL-BOUND ALBUMS: These books contain a fixed number of pages, so are perfect for finite projects, such as gift or vacation albums. Although pages can be removed by simply ripping them out, they cannot be inserted or reinserted. Spiral-bound books are easy to work with because they lie flat against the work surface.

POST-BOUND ALBUMS: Similar to three-ring binders, these books allow you to add or rearrange pages by lifting them on and off the binding posts. Some post-bound albums come with a starter set of pages. Refills and page protectors are sold separately.

STRAP-STYLE ALBUMS: Plastic straps woven through sturdy staples and attached to the pages help this album lie flat when opened. The facing pages lie close together, making them perfect for two-page layouts or pop-up spreads.

PHOTO-MOUNTING METHODS
AND MATERIALS

here are two photo-mounting methods to chose from: permanent and nonpermanent.

PERMANENT MOUNTING: If you want the materials you are placing in the scrapbook to remain there indefinitely, permanent mounting is your best option. Permanently mounted photos and memorabilia will remain in the book whether it is opened flat or held upright.

NONPERMANENT MOUNTING: You may wish to mount antique or heirloom photos and documents so that they can be lifted from the album pages at a later date—perhaps to have them restored or copied. Nonpermanent mounting methods hold materials on the pages without an adhesive applied directly to the photo. This method is preferred by conservators and curators.

When looking for safe scrapbooking glues or tapes be sure the product has the words "acid-free" and "photo-safe" on the label.

The world has turned quite a few times since white glue and tape were the adhesive materials of choice. Today's scrapbookers can choose from many easy and safe products that won't yellow or damage photos. All products that come in contact with photos should be acid-free, lignin-free, and PVC-free.

DOUBLE-SIDED TAPE: Simply drag the handy dispenser across the back of the photograph to lay down a strip of tape. Then adhere the photo to a mat or directly onto the page.

GLUE STICKS, PENS, AND WANDS: These tidy hand-held applicators dispense small amounts of liquid adhesive. Simply dot or dab them onto the back of the photo or mat and stick it in place. Most glue sticks are considered permanent, but "two-way glues" allow you to move a photo after placement. Two-way glues are colored when they're first dispensed, then turn clear after a few moments. If you adhere a photo to a page while the glue is still colored, the photo will be permanently mounted. If you wait and adhere it when the glue is clear, the photo can be lifted and repositioned. Two-way glues allow scrapbookers to place their photos, reassess the visual effect later, and make final adjustments.

PHOTO SPLITS ADHESIVE: This tape has a protective backing that can easily be removed using your fingertips or a craft knife. Stick one side of the split tape to the photo, remove the backing, and apply the photo to the page.

The most familiar nonpermanent mounting technique is that of photo corners. For a hand-made look, try decorating plain photo corners with small punches, drawings, or cut-out stamped designs. Change ink and embossing colors for a variety of looks.

PHOTO CORNERS: These paper or plastic triangular pockets are applied to the album page so that they correspond to the shape of the photograph. Then each corner of the photograph is slipped inside a pocket. Some photo corners need to be moistened; others have a peel-off backing. Photo corners are available in a range of sizes and colors, styles, or shapes—or, make your own.

PHOTO SLEEVES: These clear, plastic PVC-free holders resemble open-ended pillowcases. The sleeves are mounted to an album page with clear tape or photo corners. Your photos and memorabilia are then slipped inside.

SCRAPBOOKER'S TIPS

—from Marilyn Garner, San Diego, California

MAKE YOUR OWN PHOTO CORNERS
1. Cut an L-shaped piece of paper out of acid-free stock.

2. Fold each leg of the L into a corner pocket.
3. Punch or decorate corners as desired.

THE RIGHT PAPER

Paper is an essential ingredient in your creative scrapbooks. The most basic technique you will use in your book is matting your photos. Photo-safe papers come in hundreds of colors and patterns to match your specific subject matter or color scheme. To be photo-safe like your album page, the paper should be pH neutral (acid-free). Many varieties also come buffered and lignin-free.

These plastic sheaths protect album pages from fingerprints, grease, dust, spills, smudges, and abrasions. They also separate nonarchival-quality products from photos on facing pages. Photo sleeves make it possible for you to view documents or images from both sides.

PENS, MARKERS, AND PENCILS

〰

When decorating pages or "journaling" with words and stories, always use pens and markers that are permanent and lightfast. Pigment inks resist fading. Look for pigment pens and markers that are labeled as "fade-resistant," "colorfast," "pH balanced," and "waterproof."

PIGMENT PENS: A scrapbooker's most essential writing tools are pigment pens. They come in a variety of colors with assorted tips. Calligraphy markers have flat felt tips that angle the letters, helping to create scroll-like effects.

PENCILS: Use only wax-based pencils when writing on the backs of photos. For decorative embellishments, use artist-quality colored pencils.

DYE-BASED MARKERS: These markers are similar to felt-tipped markers, but contain dye ink that is not lightfast, although they should last a long time in a closed album. These markers work well with stamping and other decorative touches, but are not recommended for journaling.

HANDCOLORING PENS AND PAINTS: Use these pens or paints to tint black-and-white photos. The color you brush onto the picture penetrates the print emulsion.

PHOTO-SAFE SUPPLIES

❖ *PAPER (scrapbook pages, papers, die cuts, frames): Acid-free (pH between 7 and 8.5), lignin-free, and preferably buffered.*

❖ *PAGE PROTECTORS and other plastic products: PVC-free.*

❖ *ADHESIVES AND MOUNTS: Acid-free and photo-safe.*

❖ *PENS AND MARKERS: Pigment ink that is lightfast and fade-resistant, waterproof, and colorfast.*

❖ *PENCILS: Wax-based pencils to mark the backs of photos. Artist-quality colored pencils for decorative embellishments on paper*

▷ *FLOWER GIRL. Artist: Rosemary Bluhm.*
A hand-tinted touch is added to a black-and-white photo. The page is brought to life with stamps and markers, printed paper, and a springtime border.

June, 1997

Jimmy & Gigi

Jimmy is 3½ years old and has an imaginary friend. One beautiful sunny morning he said "Mommy can we take a picture of Gigi so I can always remember him?" Here is the result in Jim's own words:

Gigi is a little tiny baby penguin. He is my friend. I met him at daycare last year. Sometimes he has to go home to his Mommy & Daddy. They live at the North Pole. We like to play Penguin Shuffle & we like to eat macaroni. Gigi also likes to eat fish. He's my very, very sweet baby & I love him!

SPECIAL TOOLS AND METHODS

~~~

Through the years, scrapbook albums have evolved from simple journals to keepsake works of art. Scrapbookers continue to explore new ways to record their memories and create albums that are as unique as they are. Here are some of the many materials and methods you can use alone or in combination to create your one-of-a-kind album. You may discover others, too. Use your imagination. There are no limits to your creativity!

STICKERS

~~~

Stickers are colorful, fun, and affordable. They light up a page, cover up mistakes, and add supporting illustrations and details to the page. Stickers make wonderful corners, frames, and mats. They can also be applied in patterns along the edges of a page or a mat to make simple, decorative borders.

Stickers come in lots of colors and sizes and the number of available designs are almost too numerous to believe. Because stickers are so easy to use—you just peel off the backing and stick—it's easy for beginners to overuse them.

◁ *JIMMY AND GIGI. Artist: Lisa Dixon.*
A mother's love is shown in many ways. Honoring the process of growing up is one of the most touching. The wonderful summertime image of Jimmy and his imaginary friend Gigi, a small penguin, is preserved on a cheerful page complemented with photos cropped with heart templates, stickers, and simple journaling.

▷ *TRUE LOVE. Artist: Marilyn Garner.*
Stickers are a quick and easy way to add color and style to an album page. String a garland of candy hearts using a wavy ruler to draw the string and heart templates to cut out the corner hearts. Cut the angels and banner title free-hand. Embellish with sticker letters and colored pens.

HOPSCOTCH. Artist: Kim Buckley.
Hop. swing, ride, run, these numbered pages are plain fun! Simple verse and brightly colored number die cuts or stencils add to an up-beat day-at-the-park spread. Geometric stickers, colored pens, and oval templates make the job as easy as 1-2-3.

The key to good sticker art, however, is moderation. Think of a sticker as an ornamental pin—although one pin, or even two, can make the outfit, too many can look gaudy. Likewise, too many stickers clutter and detract from the page rather than add interest and appeal.

After you have mounted your photographs and memorabilia on the album page and finished whatever journaling you wish to do, select the stickers you want to add for embellishment. It's a good idea to experiment with the placement before adhering them to the page—once the backing is removed and stickers are applied to the page, they are permanently in place. To protect your photos, place stickers where they won't come in contact with the photos.

STAMPS

～

*H*ow can something so simple create such complex and impressive results? That's the beauty of stamps. With a rubber stamp and an ink pad, you can make delicate borders, lacy photo corners, stamped backgrounds, and eye-catching mats. And working with colored inks and colored pens or markers can vary the special effects.

To begin stamping, tap the rubber side of the stamp on the ink pad. Be sure the stamp is evenly covered with ink. If your stamp image is larger than the ink pad, or if you want to use more than one color, ink the stamp with colored markers. Apply the stamp to the paper before the ink dries. Press down firmly. Do not rock or wiggle the stamp, or the image may blur.

Ink from dye ink pads dries immediately, however pigment inks take up to twenty-four hours to air-dry. You can speed up the drying process somewhat by holding the stamped paper close to a heat source, such as a toaster or hot plate, for several minutes. There are also heat guns available that are specifically made for setting ink. Heat guns are the best option.

Stamping is perfect for creating unique mats or background designs on album pages. Stamps also make wonderful border designs. Just be sure to practice several times before trying this great effect on your scrapbook pages.

There are hundreds of different types of rubber stamps to choose

SNOWFLAKES.
Artist: Gayleen Spiros.
Randomly stamped backgrounds require little precision. Stamp your designs right off the page to create a seamless look to the design. For a special accent, color in the images with markers or pencils.

SABRINA. Artist: Cindy Inloes. Stamps and stickers are often used together on a scrapbook page. Give a large portrait center stage at a jaunty angle and support it by a handful of small images arranged to create a natural-looking border. Trim the large portrait with fancy scissors. Mat with colored paper trimmed with fancy scissors. Freehand-cut "photo corners" from black paper. Crop smaller proof shots and mount with stickers (or stamped art) along the border.

from. Select those you like best or the ones that will support your theme.

Here are just a few of the many styles of stamps available, along with some ideas on how to use them:

- ❖ *Alphabet or word stamps:* to create distinctive lettering.
- ❖ *Border stamps* (long designs): for decorating the edges of pages.
- ❖ *Corner stamps:* for decorating the corners of pages.
- ❖ *Mini-stamps* (less than $1/2$ inch in diameter).
- ❖ *Photo-corner stamps:* for decorating the corners of photographs.
- ❖ *Photo-frame stamps* (large frame-shaped stamps with an empty center): for framing photographs.
- ❖ *Roller stamps* (imprinted on a wheel): to create lines of patterns.
- ❖ *Theme stamps* (available for every topic, from quilting, music, and gardening to sewing, animals, and sports): to add illustrations and details to support the theme of your album.

HEAT EMBOSSING

A stamped image by itself is attractive, but when you emboss that image it becomes more significant. Embossing is not difficult when you have the right tools and the result is very effective. You can emboss an image or letters. Before mounting any photographs on the page, stamp or draw the images that you want to emboss, using embossing ink. Choose an opaque or clear embossing powder. Opaque powders conceal the color of the ink; clear powders allow the color to show through. Iridescent pearl and sparkle powders are also available.

 ❖ Liberally cover the inked area with the embossing powder.
 ❖ Tap any excess powder off the image and back into the container.
 ❖ Apply heat from a toaster, hot plate, or heat gun until the ink in the powder rises and shines.
 ❖ Once the images are dried, mount the photographs on the page. (You should never expose photos to heat.)
 ❖ Cover the embossed pages with page protectors to prevent them from rubbing against the facing pages.

Embossed letters are an elegant way to decorate your album cover or title page. To create illuminated letters, you need an embossing pen, gold embossing powder, a heat source, and a method to add color to your design. You could draw a letter freehand or copy one from a book or magazine. Using an embossing pen, draw over the letter and fill in the areas of the letter you want to emboss. Sprinkle embossing powder over the embossing ink and tap off the excess powder. Apply heat to create the raised embossed image. It can then be colored with watercolors, markers, or colored pencils. Experiment with calligraphy pens to complete the page.

PUNCHES

~~~

T he ancient Oriental art of paper-cutting has met its twentieth-century match! With colored paper and punch tools, there are hundreds of ways to create interesting designs for your album pages. With these easy-to-use little tools, you can cut sections of paper in a variety of shapes, leaving precise designs in your scrapbook pages. They can also be used to punch patterns and shapes from contrasting paper.

It's easy to get punch-happy when playing with the many types of punches that are available. Here's a description of some of them:

FLOWER BORDERS. Artist: Elizabeth Harward.
These colorful rhythmic floral borders are made using a single heart punch. The flowers are four hearts, the buds are a single inverted heart. The leaves are halved hearts.

- ❖ *Basic punch:* creates die-cut shapes (ranging in size from small to jumbo).
- ❖ *Border punch:* cuts long decorative borders along straight edges.
- ❖ *Corner lace punch:* cuts corner edges into delicate lace patterns or other decorative designs.
- ❖ *Corner rounder and corner-decoration rounder punch:* cuts corners and cuts patterns in corners while also rounding.
- ❖ *Double punch:* two punches on one punch pallet.
- ❖ *Extension punch:* A long-handled punch, for reaching deep into the interior areas of the paper.
- ❖ *Frame punch:* creates framed images.
- ❖ *Hand-held punch:* scissors-like punch, similar to a one-hole office punch, that cuts tiny images.
- ❖ *Silhouette punch:* removes the background around an image, leaving a framed silhouette.

BUILDING PUNCHED SHAPES

A punched design can add whimsy to a page, turn straight edges into lacy doilies, or create beautiful borders for mats and frames. But the real fun begins when you start layering punched shapes to make your own unique creations. By building and stacking, simple punched shapes can become interesting multi-dimensional forms.

To make a punch sculpture:

- ❖ Insert the paper into the mouth of the punch.
- ❖ Press down on the punch firmly.
- ❖ Carefully remove the punched-out piece of paper.
- ❖ Continue working around the page until you have punched out all the shapes you need.
- ❖ Assemble punched-out shapes to make a three-dimensional object.
- ❖ Adhere the object to the scrapbook page with adhesive.

FLOWER PUNCH. Artists: Pam Klassen and Joyce Feil.
Punch shapes can be layered and combined to create beautiful images from nature like this floral bouquet.

GLENDALE FARMS.
Artist: Erica Pierovich.
A sunny autumn day is preserved here with simple photos under a shower of colorful falling leaves created with oak, birch, and maple punches in various sizes. Punched shapes can be used singly or in groups for a dimensional effect, or amassed into a more sculptural image.

Decide on the object you wish to create—a flower or bird, for example. Next, think about the basic shapes that make up that object and the type of punches that you'll need to make those shapes. A bird has a body (an upside-down heart), a head (a circle), beak (cut star), wings (cut birch leaf), and feet (cut snowflakes). Punch the shapes you need. Assemble them with a small amount of adhesive. A tweezer is helpful for handling very small elements. Once the object is finished, apply it to the scrapbook page.

Don't allow a limited punch collection to limit your fun. If you don't have a punch with the desired shape, either hand-cut the piece with scissors, or use a portion of another punched shape. For example, one half of a punched sun can become an eyelid (complete with lashes), or, when flipped upside down, a crazy head of hair.

PUNCHING PROBLEMS ?

MY PUNCH IS STICKING!
Solution: *Punch several times through waxed paper or apply a light coat of oil to the surface of the punch. Before you begin to work on your scrapbook again, be sure to remove oil residue by punching through scrap paper several times.*

I CAN'T GET THROUGH THE PAPER!
Solution: *Put the punch on the ground and gently step on it. If this doesn't work, choose thinner paper.*

THE PUNCHED SHAPE NEVER ENDS UP WHERE I WANT IT!
Solution: *Draw lines or a simple graph on the back of the paper. Insert the paper into* the mouth of the punch. Turn the punch and paper over to check that the punch is correctly positioned over your drawing.

I DON'T HAVE ENOUGH PUNCHES FOR MY PROJECTS!
Solution: *Throw a punching party. Invite friends to bring their punches. Punch numerous shapes with the "visiting" punches and store them until needed.*

To prevent punches from sticking, punch often through standard waxed paper.

△ CROW. Artist: Tonya Jeppson.
The crow was created from five basic shapes: the body (inverted heart), head (circle), beak (cut star), wings (halves of birch leaf), and feet (cut snowflake). By putting basic shapes together in different ways you can create unique new forms.

▷ (overleaf) TIPTOE THROUGH THE TULIPS.
Artist: Loy Stevens.
Colored pens, tulip die cuts, and oval templates made this joyous scrapbook page. Lay the tulip die cut on top of cropped ovals, trace, and cut out. The reverse silhouette adds an unusual note.

Tiptoe through the

Lucille

Ross

& Joan

Lil' TULIP TOWN U.S.A.

SKAGIT VALLEY BULB FARM

DIE CUTS

*H*ow did we ever do without die cuts? Die cuts—precut paper shapes in printed and in solid colors—have become such a part of modern scrapbooking that it's almost impossible to imagine creating an album without them. These decorative paper shapes are great for adding theme accents to a page, as mats for photos, and as surfaces for journaling. You can crop photos into die-cut shapes for special effects, too. Some die cuts are available with adhesive backs—just peel off the protective liner and stick!

To mat a photo, select a die cut that complements the photo's color and character. Adhere the photo to the die cut or place the photo behind a die-cut window (as in the page illustrated here), and then attach it to the album page. You could also mat the die cut on another paper or die cut to add more dimension.

Journaling on die cuts sets off the text as an important element on the page. And, best of all, if you make an error while writing on a die cut, you can simply throw the die cut away and begin again, without ruining the album page. Like stickers, die cuts are also useful for covering up any mistakes.

Some stores will create customized die cuts, using the paper of your choice. Or, cut your own die using a template and your favorite paper.

◁ YOU ARE MY SUNSHINE. *Artist: Sandi Genovese.*
A banner die cut and garden-theme cut-outs were all the tools needed to create this garden. The flower die cuts frame the photos of the children's faces, which beam out from under the flower centers.

△ 4TH OF JULY. *Artist: Diana Stamos.*
Crop some photos into flag shapes using a wavy ruler. Crop other photos and stars with templates. Draw a border around the edges of the page. Accent finishing touches with a title and flag stickers.

TEMPLATES

A template is a pattern that is often made of plastic, but may also be sturdy paper or cardboard. Whether you buy them or make your own, templates have a multitude of uses. You can trace around them to make die cuts, or trace their shapes onto photos as a guide for cropping (clear plastic templates make it easier to see which areas to crop).

There are templates that help you create everything from large frames to flourish accents. Some rulers include fancy template edges for turning the sides of album pages into waves or patterns.

Templates can also be used as guides for journaling. Trace around the template and then journal along the line to give the block of words a particular shape. You can also journal to fill in the traced area. These techniques add novelty to your pages and are more fun than following ruler-straight lines.

Template shapes vary—from hearts and animals to letters, numbers, and simple geometric patterns. With templates in hand, any album artist can turn boxy, rectangular photos and mats into something special.

It is not difficult to custom-make your own template. Try a simple one to start:

❖ Cut off the edges of a large, plastic lid (from a coffee can, for example) so that you are left with a flat disk.

❖ Find an object or design with a simple shape (try a cookie cutter).

❖ Trace the shape on a piece of paper.

❖ Place the paper over the plastic lid on a cutting mat (or even tape available at art supply stores).

❖ With a craft knife or scissors cut through the paper and the plastic, following the shape of the design.

❖ Remove the paper, and your plastic template is ready to use.

Ready-made templates are available in many different shapes and sizes.

FRAMES

~~~

Frame your photos and put them away—in your scrapbook, that is! You can create your own frames from original artwork or cutout designs. Or you can choose from the large selection of commercially produced scrapbook frames, which range in shape and style from classical to whimsical. Just remember only to buy frames made with acid- and lignin-free materials (see page 24).

Commercially produced frames offer an easy alternative to matting. Just slip your photo behind the frame and mount it in your album. Frames are especially effective for creating a formal look for historical photographs, portraits, and wedding albums!

SCISSORS AND RULERS

~~~

Standard-style scissors and rulers will be a great help when assembling your scrapbook pages. But you can also create a variety of special effects with fancier versions of these basic tools. Many kinds of scissors are available with decorative blades that allow you to create scalloped, jagged, or lacy patterns. There are even scissors that create deckle edges similar to those on very old photos. Special scissors are also available to help you cut rounded and decorative corners.

Rulers are easy to use and perfect for creating straight edges along photos, mats, and album

▷ *CATCHIN' SOME ZZZZ'S. Artist: Kristi Hazelrigg.*
Sleepytime photographs of a child are cropped into Z's with the help of a straight-edged ruler and scissors.

▷▷ *(Overleaf) GOING FOR A DIP AT GRANDMA'S HOUSE. Artist: Tammy Layman.*
Square and round templates help crop photos effectively, with the help of straight-edged scissors, and aquatic stickers add a humorous touch to an underwater scrapbook page.

Going For A Dip At Grandmas House

pages. Decorative rulers work well as templates, making it easy to trace and cut patterns too complex to draw free-hand. Look in your local art supply store for special scissors and special papers to use for backgrounds, mats, or frames.

◁ *A sampling of the many varieties of interesting papers available at craft and art supply stores.*

▷ WEDDING PORTRAIT. *Artist: Joyce Feil. A stunning paper cut-out frame created by the artist for a formal wedding portrait of Amy Gilbert.*

TIPS FOR STORING SCRAPBOOK SUPPLIES

You can invest in one of the commercial storage systems that are made just for scrapbooking supplies. Or try some of these simple storage tips:

❖ *Keep photos in photo-safe boxes stored in a dark, dry place. Photographs should not come into contact with rubber bands, paper clips, or cellophane and masking tape.*

❖ *Store loose punched shapes in plastic storage boxes, sewing kits, spice drawers, or dental-floss boxes. Label each box to make it easier to find the designs when you need them.*

❖ *Store scissors and templates in a sewing box or plastic bin.*

❖ *Store paper, die cuts, and stickers in hanging folders in a file cabinet, in baseball-card holders, or notebooks with plastic (PVC-free) top-loading pages.*

❖ *Store adhesives in sealable plastic bags. Keep them separate from other scrapbooking supplies.*

❖ *Store albums so that they are standing upright and away from moisture and direct sunlight.*

Amy Gilbert
Wed to Curtiss Schnur
May 27, 1995

He liked helping Dad garden so the sunflowers are...

Mack has provided us with so many wonderful memories. The picture of him asleep at the table was from a week-long visit when he was 22 mo's old. We took him to Yuma to visit Nana & Grandpa Winkler; he entertained Grandpa by stacking all the creamers over & over. (He likes to build & has a great imagination). His favorite game was a roll of toilet paper that he kept putting his animals thru. Another fun time was running thru the sprinklers out front. When the dogs ate his onesie, he kept saying De ate it! but he cried when he saw his socks demolished.

JOURNALING

~~~

*H*ow often have you found yourself staring at a photo, sifting frantically through your memory for some clue that will help you place it? The person eating the hot dog looks vaguely familiar. The beach in the background rings a bell. The children look older than toddlers, but younger than kindergartners. Through a long process of elimination, you may zero in on the time and place that the photo was taken, but its significance may still elude you. There's no better argument in support of journaling!

CONTEXT

Whether in the form of short notes or longer entries and stories, journaling supplies the background context for your scrapbook page. Long after the film has been developed and the photo has found a home within your album, your journaling will help you remember why you were inspired to focus on and click that particular shot.

Journaling also provides the voice behind the images. Who you are is reflected in the way you choose to journal. The style and words you choose set the tone for the page and the album. For example, the journaling in your heritage album may be formal, with complete sentences and precise vocabulary; journaling in a child's album may be in the form of incomplete sentences—or even baby talk.

There are four basic approaches to journaling:

BULLETS—A brief form of journaling that supplies only the most basic information—*who, what, when,* and *where*. For example:

Mary Smith. Age 5. Albuquerque, New Mexico. Grandma's house. 7-4-97.

CAPTIONING—These longer labels present some or all of the basic information covered in bullets, but in complete sentences rather than fragments. Captions also present the opportunity for more creative expression. The same information as above, but in caption form might read:

Mary Smith was five years old when this picture was taken. She was vacationing at her grandma's house in Albuquerque, New Mexico, over the Fourth of July weekend. What a great barbecue we had!

HANGING OUT TO DRY. Artist: Pat Brooks.
Photos cropped and layered into imaginative and playful shapes add a touch of whimsy and provide a strong visual element for this well-captioned page. Sunflowers smile at this little fellow's antics that are hung out for all to see.

John & Nancy Johnson

Married: February 15, 1892 at the Piney Grove Baptist Church by her father — **John Collette**

- ♥ "I guess my mother and father thought their children were lucky to have grown up without ever getting into trouble that could not be handled."

- ♥ "Although, there was a lot of sorry — with my oldest sister, Carrie, dying of cancer at age 31, leaving three little children — my brother, Lee, getting killed in the coal mines in 1930 at age 30, leaving two children — my oldest brother, Bob, joining the Army during World War I, at age 17. Lots of heartache and sorry."

- ♥ "Then, as mother told me, I have our grandchildren we love, to sorry about now. She would "pray, ask God. to watch over and protect them."

JOHNSON

Janet
Dec. 2, 1908

- Christened as Maude, but when her friend Janet Gaynor, she changed it. Our brother Bob was glad, he thought Maude sounded said she looked like like the name of a horse.
- Janet eloped with Arthur Prichard at the age of 17. The next day she saw our dad and started crying when she realized she couldn't go home.
- I didn't like Arthur for the longest time. ~ cause he took my sissie away from me.
- They remained married for over fifty years! They had one son: Charles.

Lora Lee & Cora

Cora
Jan. 5, 1913   June 16, 1982

- I went to school with Cora and Virginia for a few years, they were closest to my age.
- Cora ran away on decoration day (Memorial Day) and eloped with Ed Lefevers ~ at age 14! The rest of us had gone to the cemetary for the services. Once Dad found out, he tried to catch them on horseback ~ but he was too late.
- Ed was later killed by "ruffians" when Cora was pregnant with Loretta. She moved home with us.
- 2nd husband, Charlie Sampson, died of a stroke. Together they had a daughter: Ada.
- 3rd husband, Gil Davis, and Cora then had: Kenneth, Bonnie, Jenny, and Frank.
- Cora raised her granddaughter, Lora Lee, who was abandoned by her mother.

Cora

STORYTELLING—A longer form of journaling that includes the basic information, but also adds additional details, sets a mood, and provides a narrator's voice. Storytelling puts the photo in a context by explaining what happened before and after the photo was taken. Sometimes the memories are only indirectly related to the photograph. The same barbecue, as a story, might read:

"Are we there yet?" Mary almost drove us crazy, asking us that every five minutes all the way from Denver to Albuquerque! We'd explained that the drive would take us two days, but to a five-year-old, time really has no significance. So, we tried to keep her busy with car games (we must have played the alphabet game a hundred times!). When we finally got to Grandma's house, Mary barreled out of the car and almost knocked Mom down with hugs. Dad had the grill going, and the traditional Fourth of July shish kebabs were cooking away.

◁ *GRANDMA JOHNSON.*
Artist: Janet Morrison.
A family history full of interesting stories needed to be told. Storytelling, old photographs of Grannie and her family, and a page dedicated to each of Grannie's ten brothers and sisters are included in this album. In the artist's words: "I wrote out the jounaling in Grannie's voice, the way she told the stories to me. I wrote in pencil first to make sure the text fit, then wrote over the penciled text using embellished lettering."

▷ *CAMPING IN THE MOONLIGHT.*
Artist: Claire Dozier-Seckel.
Die cuts and paper-punched stars, colored paper, and a trusty black pen with which to caption the page help make this album insert a fitting memory of a family's first camping trip.

Denali Alyeska - our little cherub!

May
1997

These are a few of our favorite things ♫:
"bella bionda", pure white calla lilies & swans,
mother & daughter
dresses, lush green
countryside, birds
singing, summertime
sounds & scents!

It reminded me of all those Fourth of Julys during my childhood. Sometimes we celebrated them at home and sometimes we took trips, but wherever we were, Dad made shish kebabs. I remember the year that the dog snatched them right off the grill, and Dad had to go down to the grocery store because he refused to substitute hamburgers or hot dogs (which we had in the refrigerator). Nope. The Fourth of July just wouldn't be the Fourth of July without shish kebabs!

POETIC JOURNALING—This form of journaling relies on meaningful song lyrics, Bible verses, or poems to capture the mood of the page. Poetic journaling is a natural choice for historical albums, holiday albums, wedding albums, and inspirational themes. You might consider using songs from the period to complement historical albums, or add carols to your Christmas scrapbook. Beautifully handwritten copies of the wedding vows—perhaps using decorative lettering—add a deeply personal touch to the pages of a wedding album.

DECORATIVE LETTERING

So, you got C's in penmanship in elementary school and have shied away from writing ever since? That's no excuse to shy away from lettering within your scrapbook! While beautiful handwriting is a plus, even those with less-than-perfect script can enhance their scrapbook pages with journaling or decorative lettering. Lettering templates and the wide selection of calligraphy and decorative pen tips make the job easier. There are also some wonderful lettering instruction books that are on the market.

If you're still nervous about your aptitude, type out the message or journaling information on a computer using a decorative font and print out the page. Place the printout on a light table, position your scrapbook page over it, and trace the letters. Before you know it, you'll gain confidence, and the words will be flowing from your fingertips—just like ink from a pen.

In addition to journaling, you can use decorative lettering to add an extra design element to your album pages. Add letters within shapes, using a template as a guide—write either within the borders of the shape or around the perimeter. Or include decorative messages as borders or as "streamers" across the page.

◁ *(previous page)* OUR FAVORITE THINGS.
Artist: Melody Sperl.
Poetic journaling is complemented beautifully by poetic images photographed in an idyllic peaceful place. Templates, fancy scissors, and colored paper all contribute to the magical feeling.

▷ SUNBEAMS.
Artist: Pat Murray.
A close-cropped photo is matted and mounted on a page filled with the sun's rays. Poem verses are written in beautiful calligraphy and matted before being placed on the page.

TITLE PAGES

A title page creates the viewer's first impression of your scrapbook. It can stimulate interest, convey the tone, and establish a theme or style. Whether it's elegant or whimsical, the title page prepares the reader for the contents of the album. A clean, open page with a simple title and minimal adornment works best. Practice your lettering before committing pen to album page. For a more dramatic effect, draw the letters of the title onto a separate piece of paper, cut the letters out, and mount them on the page. You can also use letter die cuts or letter stickers.

Consider mixing media, too. A flutter of ribbon, a swatch of lace, or a pressed flower will add simple beauty. Your title page is an invitation to enter the album and browse. Make the page unique. Make it gracious. Make it distinctly yours.

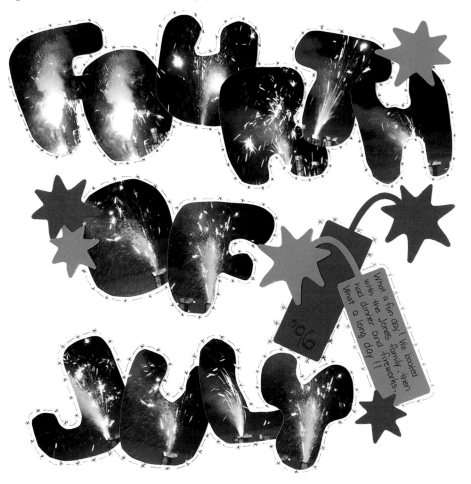

FIREWORKS. Artist: Janet Wells.
This lively page is created with letters cut freehand from photos. Mount the cut letters
on the page and outline with dashed lines and stars. Add firecracker die cuts.

MAKE A JOYFUL NOISE. Artist: Debbie Lloyd.
Compose your own sweet song with these delightful musical notes. The tools are simple—black pen and paper, a circle template, and stickers.

DESIGNING THE PAGES

~~~

*T*ake a stroll through a museum or look through the pages of an art book. While works of art may vary in subject and style, they all have some basic elements in common—a balanced composition that pleases the eye, colors that establish a mood and help tell the story, perspective and contrast to create dimension and add interest. A good scrapbook page and a beautiful album both rely on the same principles of design as other art forms. Here are some ideas to keep in mind while planning and laying out your pages.

CREATE BALANCE

*D*ecide on the centerpiece or focal point of the page. A page without a focal point can be confusing, leaving the viewer unsure where to look and unable to take in all the information. A scrapbook page may contain several images, but decide on the one that is important or interesting enough to be the primary image, supported by all the others. For example, a picture of a person may be especially compelling because the subject is looking directly into the lens, seeming to make eye contact with the viewer.

The primary image is usually placed in a central or dominant position on the page. It is often larger than the supporting pictures, too. Color can also set apart the primary image. The picture might be brighter or darker than the others on the page, or you might want to place it within a particularly distinctive mat or frame.

Primary images are emphasized and complemented by secondary, or supporting, images on the page. Usually smaller in size, these photos reinforce or play off of the subject of the primary photograph. They may even be variations on the same subject or wider views of the same shot. Photographs taken just before and after the primary photo make excellent supporting images, setting the scene for the event or moment captured in the larger photograph.

Any child knows that a sandcastle is the best when it has rectangular turrets, spiral stair-

◁ *SASHA'S HOUSE. Artist: Diane Gibbs.*
There is no question about the focal point of this colorful scrapbook page created with Mary Engelbreit style. The shapes, the colors, and the placement of elements on the page all pull us in to the starring photograph.

SUMMER CAMP. Artist: Kelly Angard.
Photos cropped in different shapes are the central point of a sunny sunburst page. Yellow paper cut in triangles form the sun's rays and die-cut letters provide the labels.

cases, triangular roofs, and circular moats. Shapes add dimension and visual interest—even on an album page. Cropped photos, colorful stickers, die-cut and punched shapes, and patterned and textured papers help break the monotony of the rectangular page.

EXPERIMENT WITH COLOR

When it comes to color, less is sometimes more. How much is too much? That's up to the album artist to decide. Color has a profound emotional effect on people. Studies have shown that blue calms us, red excites us, and yellow makes us happy. Because color is so powerful, even a small amount on a scrapbook page may affect the viewer's response—so choose color carefully.

Some color pairs work better than others, and can create a range of effects, from high contrast (for example, red and green) to balanced or very low contrast (for example, blue and green). Consult a color wheel to explore the various possibilities.

CREATIVE CROPPING

〰〰

When it comes to photographs, more isn't always better—that's why experienced scrapbookers are also experienced photo croppers. Cropping is the process of cutting photos either to enhance the image—by turning it into a unique shape, for example—or to eliminate extraneous portions of the shot.

▷ *NEW MEXICO. Artist: Stacy Julian.*
Color on a scrapbook page is meant to make your photos come alive. When choosing color for your scrapbook designs draw on the colors of your pictures. Make sure the colors you select don't overwhelm the pictures. And don't be afraid to experiment. This artist experiments with color variations in the background, mat, and borders.

▽ *SUMMER. Artists: Pam Klassen, Ron Gerbrandt based on original page and photos by Stacey Bruce.*
This witty combination of split complementary colors and triads provokes a sunny summer day remembrance. Hand-cut letters and shapes offer playful arrangements for vacationing children.

COLOR TIPS

Here are some simple guidelines to keep in mind when selecting colors for your scrapbook page:

❖ *Take cues from the primary photographs. Choose papers and other decorative elements to emphasize or complement the colors.*

❖ *Don't overpower the photos. Avoid background or decorative colors that clash with or detract attention from the photos.*

❖ *Choose colors that convey the mood of the page. For a birthday party, for example, consider using "happy" colors, such as red, yellow, or orange, instead of calm pastel blues or greens.*

❖ *Don't feel obligated to use traditional holiday colors when designing holiday pages—they may not always work.*

❖ *Don't be afraid to experiment. Trust your eye and intuition.*

The key phrase to keep in mind when cropping is "take it easy." Overly enthusiastic croppers may find themselves indiscriminately removing important portions of a photo. Before beginning to trim a photo, ask yourself these questions: Does this portion of the photo set the mood or add interest or balance to the image? Does it help the viewer date or place the photo? Will the primary image be able to stand alone if taken out of context?

Good cropping requires a steady hand, calculating eye, and, above all, courage. Practice on photos you don't love, or copies of the photos you do love. Cropping skills develop with practice.

CROPPING WITH TEMPLATES: Templates are often used to crop photos into distinct shapes to support the special theme of an album. Trace the template shape onto the photo and simply cut away the unwanted areas of the image with straight-edge or decorative scissors. The cropped photos can be used alone or assembled into a new shape.

CROPPING FREEHAND: With straight-edge or decorative scissors, you can crop photographs into numerous shapes to add decorative elements to a page. For example, a photo showing a sky lit up with fireworks may be cropped to look like a single shooting star or even into letters like the Fourth of July sample on page 60; a photo showing a garden filled with flowers may be cropped into the shape of a single blossom.

SILHOUETTING: Silhouetting is usually a freehand operation. To silhouette an image, the album artist cuts away the surrounding background, leaving only the primary subject. A silhouette looks like a paper doll of the subject. The silhouette can either be mounted, combined with other images, or applied directly to the album page.

▷ *YOU'RE UNBELIEVABLE. Artist: Norma Bauman. Different-sized photo prints create a dramatic effect in this progressive slam dunk series. Silhouette all but the largest print. Mount silhouetted photos on the large print, arranged from largest to smallest. Finally, accent your page with stars and journaling.*

◁ *KAMP AT K-KOUNTRY. Artist: Mary Browder. Cropping photos to fit a template can "correct" crooked or uneven photos! For this design, photocopy and enlarge an illustration to create your own template for a wagon-wheel spoke. Crop photos using the template, and arrange appropriately. Cut a circle for the center.*

CROPPING WITH THE CAMERA

It's true. A multitude of photo problems can be corrected with a little skill and a pair of scissors. But it's better simply to take the best photos to begin with. Here are some tips for shooting photographs that won't need cropping:

❖ *Frame the subject carefully as you look through the viewfinder.*

❖ *Zoom in as close as possible—or move closer to the subject as necessary before snapping the shutter.*

❖ *Fill the frame with the primary image.*

❖ *Photograph people at eye level to create a sense of intimacy.*

DECORATIVE MATS

With scissors, adhesives, paper, and templates, a scrapbooker can create the perfect "home" for photographs. A mat around a photo sets off the image, focuses the viewer's attention, and adds interest and balance to the album page. To create a mat, adhere the photo to a piece of paper. Cut a paper border of the width and shape you want around the edges of the photograph using straight-edge or decorative scissors. If you still need to crop the photo, do so before you cut the mat.

Some scrapbookers crop a photo with a template, then they cut a mat for the photo with a larger template of a similar shape. For other special effects, consider matting a round photo on a square mat, or silhouette a cropped photo on a round mat.

Double-matting adds extra visual interest. Simply mat the photo as described above, and then adhere the matted photo to another piece of paper of a contrasting or complementary color. Cut the larger mat to the desired size and adhere it to the album page. Or add one or two additional mats to it first to add extra dimension.

Borders seem to say, "Within, you'll find something wonderful!" Whether made with stamps, punches, inks, stickers, ribbons, die cuts, or photographs, borders add a special finishing touch to any scrapbook page.

△ *A Rose By Any Other Name. Artist: Debbie Hewitt.*
Nothing could be sweeter than a little girl wrapped in a gar-
land of flowers. Photos are matted with printed and colored
paper trimmed with fancy scissors. A wavy ruler serves as a
template for cutting wavy strips of paper. Intertwined strips
frame the page. Flower stickers add splashes of color and
carry out the theme. The soft black-and-white photos are
beautifully complemented with hand-tinted accents of pink
and green flowers. The garland border and mats
reiterate the two colors used to hand-tint the photos.

▷ *Purple Quilt. Artist: Dayna Silva.*
A page exhibiting elegant symmetry from an artist with
a degree in chemistry and biology. Cut a 3-inch strip of
lavender paper and mount across the center of the
page. Cut an 8-inch square of paper into two triangles.
Mount the pink triangles above and below the laven-
der strip. Cut two 5 1/2-inch squares into two trian-
gles and mount in the corners. Crop photos into 1
and 1 1/2-inch squares; arrange as shown.

CREATIVE PHOTO MONTAGES

There is power in numbers—that's what makes a photo montage so exciting. In a montage, photos are combined to create a single, dramatic image. The photos may be either overlapped or cropped to fit like puzzle pieces, then adhered to paper. The paper can then be cropped into a decorative shape—wedding pictures in the shape of a church bell, for example, or soccer photos in the shape of a ball—before being mounted on the scrapbook page.

△ *TOPIARIES. Artist: Marilyn Garner.*
Photos of children dressed in summer finery are wittily showcased in template-cropped images mounted into topiary-shaped plants. Punched hearts cut in half create leaves that accent the topiaries.

◁ *HEART QUILT. Artist: Marilyn Garner.*
Heart templates provide the dominant mats on this dramatic scrapbook page. Heart templates are used to crop the photos and to create mats for decorative touches. Special paper and wavy scissors are used to add color and detail to strong graphic images. The green vine-with-red-berries-border made with a medium heart and hole punches frames the page beautifully.

▷ *SHELL BEACH. Artist: Carey VanDruff.*
Create this easy puzzle page by cropping the central photo with an oval template, then arrange the remaining photos underneath and trim the overlapping edges. The artist made templates for the three shapes used here from old manila folders and shared them with her scrapbooking colleagues.

△ WET MITTENS. Artist: Lisa Garnett.
This effective red-and-white gingham border is cut from printed paper using wavy-edged scissors. Placed on top of a snow-like paper, the die-cut mittens containing oval cropped photos are hung up to dry. What an eloquent way to revive our memories of afternoons in the snow.

▷ PUMPKIN MONTAGE. Artist: Peggy Thoren.
A large pumpkin shape is filled with a montage of delightful photographs woven into a shape that helps tell the story of autumn. The stamped scarecrow peeking from atop the pumpkin wears the same colors as the featured toddler.

From This
Day Forward...

That Continues Forever

THEME SCRAPBOOKS

WEDDING ALBUMS

There was giddy bridesmaid laughter. There was the sheen of satin and the sound of admiring sighs, a garter slipped over a silk-clad leg, dozens of hugs distributed, an organ playing the "Wedding March"—and joy! A wedding album records all the special moments and special people that made up that very important day.

In addition to photographs of the special event, you might include photos of the days of courtship or from the couples' childhood or other meaningful points in their lives.

Enrich the pages with special details: copies of the guest list, descriptions of members of the wedding party, the menu from the rehearsal dinner and wedding reception, congratulation cards, song lyrics, the wedding vows and certificate. Newspaper announcements and gift lists, as well as garters, boutonnieres, and keepsakes from the honeymoon also add flavor. Journal about what went right and what went wrong while planning the wedding, favorite courtship moments, favorite love poems and songs. Open up your heart and let feelings flow onto the page.

◁ *WEDDING FLORAL FRAMES. Top spread: Artist: Pam Klassen, inspired by original art by Rubber Stampede. Bottom spread: Artist: Donna Kennedy. Decorative borders and cut-out portions of stamped images can also serve as photo corners.*

△ *IN FULL BLOOM. Artist: Dianne Rushing. This anniversary album page pays tribute to a love that has remained steadfast through many years of life's ups and downs. Pressed flowers, colored paper, cropped photos and journaling complete the page.*

FILLING IN THE BLANKS

Sometimes, too late, we discover that we should have taken more photos or had more prints made. If you don't have all the wedding photos you would like, consider some of these solutions:

❖ *Have photos made from family movies or videos.*

❖ *Ask friends and family for copies of the snapshots they took.*

❖ *Revisit the chapel or hall where the ceremony was held and photograph the interior—the altar, the pews, statues, or windows. Try some shots taken from the bride's and groom's perspectives.*

❖ *Restage scenes from the wedding or honeymoon trip to take photos and have fun.*

The wedding ceremony is only a beginning, so be sure to leave pages in the back of the wedding album for continuing events the couple is sure to share "from this day forth."

WEDDING ALBUM. Artist: Marie-Dominique Giraud. Inspiration is everywhere. Let the event itself help your creativity. This wedding title page features color copies of four arcs from a double wedding-ring quilt made with elegant blue and white French Provencial fabrics.

BABY ALBUMS

~

O h, baby! There's no one quite like you! A baby album is a record of the milestones of pregnancy, the wonder of birth, and those awesome "firsts"—from a child's first smile to the first toddling steps. The album can include photos, as well as sonograms, notes or journaling from birth preparation classes, hospital brochures, birth announcements, congratulatory cards, scraps of wrapping paper, and clips of downy hair from a child's first haircut.

Baby albums are often structured in chronological order, but some scrapbookers also organize pages around an event or activity. For example, pages titled "What's Up Doc?" might display photos of the infant's first visit to the pediatrician; "A Grand Old Time" might include photos of trips to grandparents' houses. The album can also be whimsical, with ABC pages, in which the scene or activity in the photos illustrates each letter of the alphabet, or nursery-rhyme pages.

HAND TALK. Artist: Kathi Leger.
Close-up photographs capture those infant hand movements that are all-too-quickly forgotton. Hand-print stickers, hand-cut letters, and stamps unify the page. A handwritten enchanted verse—"There's a kind of talk that's goin' round. Hand talk talkin's all over town. You don't use words and you don't need lips. You can say it all with your fingertips"—adds a personal touch.

Our Snow Angel, Rachel
~winter 1996

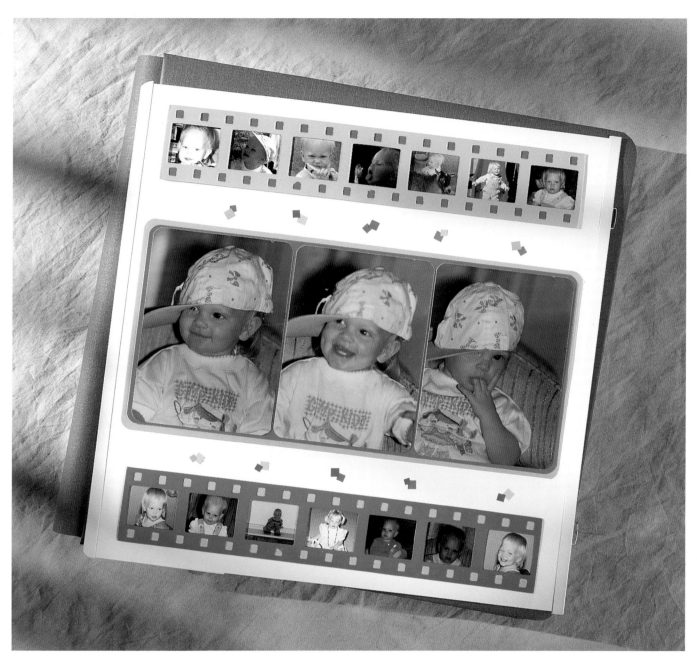

◁ STAINED-GLASS RADIANCE. *Artist: Joyce Feil.
Reminiscent of a cathedral rose window, this octagon
design incorporates a photo and colored papers. The
effect is created by precise cropping of a photo into geometric pieces. The pieces are then repositioned on contrasting paper, leaving slim margins between photo
pieces. Complementary-colored paper can be substituted
for photo segments to give the image a more realistic
cathedral-window look.*

△ LIGHTS, CAMERA, ACTION! *Artist: Debbie Schubert.
Film strips of your favorite "movie stars" are so easy to
create, and they provide years of pleasure for "stars"
and viewers alike. Use film strip die cuts out of colored
paper and mount small photos behind each frame.
Place pieces of paper of a different color behind the
holes to create some contrast. Double mat the center
photos and round the corners. Decorate with colorful
confetti stickers.*

Whatever your design, remember, that tiny face can be overwhelmed by too big a splash, so, whether you use traditional pastels or bold primaries, use color wisely and in ways that complement the child's image, rather than distract the viewer.

Journal about your pregnancy—your growing awareness of the child and your feelings about becoming a mother. Write your child a letter describing your feelings when you look at him. As the months pass, jot down information that you may forget: your child's favorite color, favorite books, the songs she sings, what makes him laugh. You'll enjoy sharing these intimate details with your child in the future.

The lovely thing about a baby album is that it is as unique as the relationship between mother and child. Putting together the album is a bit like reliving the fleeting moments of your child's earliest years. The experience is often even dearer with a bit of perspective, so wait until the baby is older—and more independent and you have a bit more time—before assembling the book. Until then, record important information—the child's weight, height, first words, first haircut, etc.—in a journal or commercially made baby book. When you are ready you can add it to your own memory album.

◁ *WHAT I LOVE ABOUT LOGAN.*
Artist: Shelley Price.
There is nothing to take the place of a mother's memories of the everyday things she enjoys about her baby. Here, in a page that is equally journal and photo page, a mother records her feelings of wondrous love for her growing baby. The simplicity of expression contributes to the warmth of the page. Stickers and a wavy border complete the design.

▷ *SPAGHETTI AND MEATBALLS.*
Artist: Joanna Barr.
Some of us need to be told to "enjoy the moment" and some of us do not. A circle template, fancy scissors, colored paper, and a wavy ruler all helped in the creation of this appealing page. Photos are cropped with the circle template and trimmed and mounted on mats cut with the wavy-edged scissors. A wavy ruler helped in making the spaghetti strands that tie the delicious photos together.

SPECIAL OCCASION ALBUMS

❧

Whether you celebrate Christmas, Chanukah, or the Chinese New Year, capture the excitement of those family holidays in a special holiday album. You're sure to have plenty of photos to choose from. Even reluctant camera bugs snap away as friends and family gather around feast tables, birthday cakes, or barbecue pits to share the year's happy moments.

◁ *COUNTDOWN TO THE HOLIDAYS.*
Artist: Pam Klassen from original idea by Kristina Holt.
Holiday stickers and a gingerbread die cut help to turn a house into an advent calendar with doors and windows that open. Don't forget to include Christmas Day on your countdown!

▷ *MORGAN'S FIRST CHRISTMAS.*
Artist: Sandra de St. Croix.
Christmases past are reawakened each year as the house is dressed for the holidays. Photos cropped and cut with fancy-edged scissors decorate these pages that are finished with stamps, stickers, and short captions. The page label announcing that this is Morgan's First Christmas at Meadow View will be a shortcut reminder in the years to come when the viewers are trying to place this Christmas in the lineup of all others.

◁ *A VALENTINE TEA PARTY.*
Artist: Kim Needham.
A wavy ruler, fancy scissors, colored pens, flower stickers, and a cupid die cut work together here to make a pretty frame for a photo of pretty little girls all dressed up for a party. Mount the photo and, with a straight ruler, draw the inner frame and with a wavy ruler draw the outer frame. Freehand-draw squiggles, dots, and hearts. Cut out a banner with fancy scissors. Decorate the banner and mount it over the photo. Place the cupid die-cut at a jaunty angle overlooking the page!

▷ *EASTER SAMPLER.*
Artist: Marilyn Garner.
Piece a patchwork of memories using colored and printed paper, Easter theme punches, fancy scissors, oval templates, and a black pen. Draw a straight-line border about one inch from the edge of the page. Make a decorative border with the bunny and heart punches. Freehand-cut tulips for page corners. Crop or silhouette photos as desired and arrange them on the page. Fill the spaces with freehand-drawn appliqué designs. Draw straight dotted lines to separate each "sampler." Draw additional details and journal with a black pen.

◁ *LADY LIBERTY.*
Artist: Shar Hiatt.
A family trip to the "Big Apple" when the Statue of Liberty was undergoing renovation under a maze of scaffolding inspired this simple page. Photos, die cuts, and colored paper are all that are needed.

HAPPY BIRTHDAY!

Blow up those balloons and ice that cake. It's time to celebrate! Birthday pages capture the excitement of that present-opening, whistle-tooting, candle-blowing event. Decorate them with festive die cuts and brightly colored mats. Crop photos into cake, balloon, and candle shapes. Create streamers and confetti from colored paper. Wrap the "package" with a birthday border.

*HAPPY BIRTHDAY.
Artist: Eileen Ruscetta.
A three-dimensional effect is accomplished by layering paper. Cover the page with colored paper. Lay one photo in the center and four photos at an angle with their inside corners touching to form a diamond. Cut paper triangles a little smaller than the triangles left between the photos. Decorate with theme stickers and streamers.*

△ THIRD BIRTHDAY. Artist: Suzanne Hall.
Turn birthday-theme printed paper, diamond template-cut photos, and birthday party memories into a pinwheel page that is pretty and action packed. Cut diamond shapes from the paper and the photos, being careful to orient the photos in the right direction. Arrange on the page as shown. Crop the center photo to fit in the hexagon shape.

▷ CREPE PARK CAROUSEL. Artist: Becky Sprague.
Cut out the carousel using a template and mount on the page. Draw in the center pole. Silhouette favorite merry-go-round photos and arrange in the carousel. Decorate with stickers.

The LARCH TREES shone like TORCHES

DONOVAN BAINEY Found a new home

Dragging the HARROWS

Cotoneaster berried Brightly

Oct 13 Excellent Kodak Seminar @ Arden

Oct as Part of Mitchell's toe removed.

Oct as PICTURE MOSAICS

October 2- Vet re. Mitchell's cat rear toe nail broken.

Landscaping @ Meadow View almonds

October 1996

The Boys go for their Walk.

OCTOBER

Tony & Larry

Visited from Halifax

SHELLAC for SHOTS - NOW - EdSM - Creative Memories Club

A SHADOWLESS NOVEMBER DAY

COMPETITIVE

CELEBRATE THE FOUR SEASONS

hink about fall. You can feel the nip in the air, hear crispy leaves crackle underfoot. Think about winter. And you can smell the fire in the fireplace, hear the silence of the snow falling. There is something special about each of the seasons that moves us. Fill your album with photos of flower gardens, pool parties, and barbecues. Decorate the pages with seasonal die cuts and templates. Add stickers with seasonal themes or punched leaves, snowflakes, suns, and flowers. Collect and photocopy flowers and leaves from your backyard, cut out the silhouettes, and mount them in your albums. There are endless ways to celebrate the seasons in a scrapbook!

The time you spend on a holiday album is a gift you give yourself. And, like most special presents, the pleasure you'll derive will remain long after the holiday has passed.

◁ *CALENDAR ALBUM. Artist: Sandra de St. Croix.*
Capture the mood of each month.

▷ *SNOWMEN AND LADY. Artist: Marilyn Garner.*
A snow couple join happy children playing on a glistening winter day.

▽ *SNOWFLAKES. Artist: Pam Klassen.*
Set a beautiful wintery mood with your own stamped photo mats using several shades of ink.

CHANGING SEASONS. Artist: Becky Carter.
Photographs of the changing seasons around the artist's home are croppped using a diamond template and then arranged into diamonds for a central quilt design. Piece the cropped photos as shown. Crop the remaining photos to fit around the diamond design. Accent with seasonal stickers, stamps, punches, and journaling.

HAPPY
Thanksgiving

Count your
blessings

Fall
1997

Be exalted, O God, above the heavens;
be over all the earth. let your glory
Psalms 57:11

s come before His presence with thanks-
and make a joyful noise unto Him with
Psalms 95:2
s.

Our week was full of

Beautiful views

Weather reports

Snowball fig

The Lexus didn't know
what hit it!

◁ *WINTER AT LAKE TAHOE. Artist: Jeanne Ciolli.*
Colored and printed paper, colored pens, and scissors are the only tools you'll need to create this favorite winter page. Photos are cropped with straight edges and mounted in the center of the page on a blue background, surrounded by trees cut out of printed paper. The house frame and roof are cut from large sheets of paper. The icicles, trees, and snow are cut freehand, as are the details on the house and the snow drifts.

▽ *AZALEA PARK. Artist: Terri Sheldon.*
An exciting way to highlight blooms and create a garden that will be in season any time of year is shown by cropping photos and piecing them together into a montage. Photos can be separated and cut into different sizes for enhanced variety.

Westminster Abbey

Since 1066 all but two of England's monarchs have been crowned here.

TRAVEL ALBUMS

~~~

Whether you find adventure around the block or around the world, it's worth recording. Travel albums record the excitement of those trips to the park, to Granny's house, or to Europe, so you can relive the event again and again. Along with other special souvenirs and memorabilia, you might want your album to include maps, brochures, hotel receipts, ticket stubs, train and plane tickets, itineraries, the names and addresses of new friends, menus, and pressed flowers and leaves. Decorate with theme die cuts, templates, stickers, and papers, or even with cut pieces of extra photos—an iris from Giverney or a tulip from Amsterdam.

The key to collecting memorabilia for your album is good planning. Before you leave home, be sure you have a way to transport the material you'll gather. A backpack with multiple zippable pockets, and a small notebook and a plastic, sealable pencil case for journaling are essential.

A journal will help you keep track of all those parks, museums, beaches, and castles. If you'll be making lots of stops, assign a number to each destination and use the same number to mark the memorabilia collected and rolls of films shot while you were there. This will help you sort the materials once you're back home.

◁ *WESTMINSTER ABBEY. Artist: Susan Sigle.*
What better way to preserve the splendor of the architecture and experiences of a trip to England than in a scrapbook? A strong page with a good focus is created by trimming a large single photograph with rounded corners and then mounting it at the base of a die-cut, silhouetted background.

△ *ENGLAND. Artist: Ron Gerbrandt.*
Cropping photos of a favorite place to be remembered adds a different dimension to this vacation page that is also part of an ABC album (the "E" here standing for England). Using travel memorabilia, contextual photography, and fun, handwritten lettering vividly recreates a sense of place.

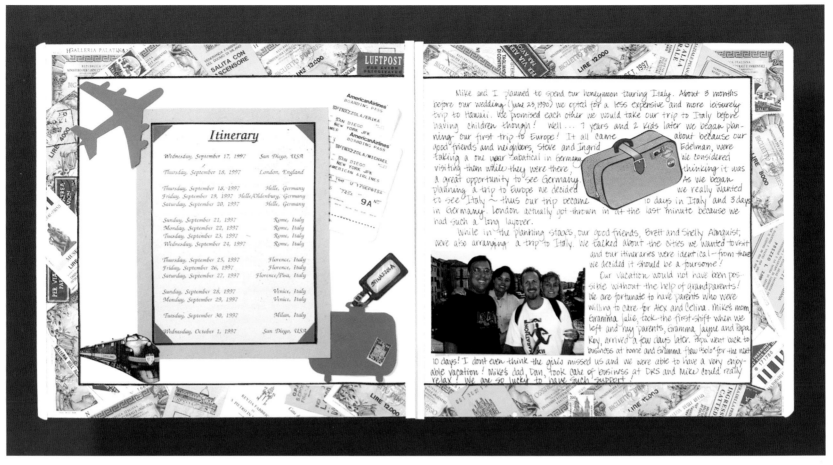

EUROPEAN VACATION. Artist: Erika Spinazzola.
Memorabilia such as money, tickets, and stamps can make a fabulous travel border with meaning that is both personal and worldly. Draw a thick black border about 1 inch from the page edge. Crop and arrange the memorabilia along the border. Mat the handwritten itinerary with colored paper, and outline with a black pen. Freehand-cut suitcase shapes. Journal with a black pen.

Journaling should include basic information about the trip—places, dates, accommodations, etc.—but also try to capture in words the sights, smells, and sounds. These descriptions will later bring back strong memories. Remember, too, that no vacation is perfect. Sometimes the things that drove us crazy during the trip make us laugh the hardest later. Write about the ups and downs.

Although a chronological organization works well for travel albums, you may want to devote pages to themes or activities: "Great Meals," "New Friends Along the Way," "Good Days and Bad Days." Try using color to tie together different phases of your trip: for example, green mats on the pages devoted to Ireland, blue pages for days at the seashore.

A travel album is a trip down memory lane. Before you've finished putting it together, you'll be itching to begin your next adventure.

HOBBY ALBUMS

～

hether they involve baseballs or golf clubs, swimsuits or toe shoes, paint or clay, those special interests and accomplishments can be documented in an album. Include photographs of you or your family members in action—with and without team-mates—and display certificates and awards. Recital programs, soccer schedules, play reviews, and sheet music all belong in a hobby album. Of course, you can't mat a trophy or mount a clay vase or afghan, but you can include them in your album. How?

PHOTOGRAPH THREE-DIMENSIONAL OR VERY LARGE OBJECTS: Set objects, such as wood-working or pottery projects, against a neutral, contrasting background in good light. Shoot the object from multiple angles and zoom in to photograph interesting details. Gardeners can record their accomplishments with photographs, too.

TAKE PHOTOS OF THE PROJECT AS IT UNFOLDS: Begin with a photograph of the tools and materials. Take a photo at each of the important stages in the process, and a photo of the finished project. Be sure to journal around the photos to add personal reflections or information.

PHOTOCOPY FLAT OBJECTS: You can reproduce embroidered or other stitched work on fabrics, sketches, small paintings, jewelry, and other relatively flat objects on a photocopy machine. For the best results, make high-quality color copies.

FILL PLASTIC POCKETS: Create or pur-chase plastic pockets in which to store small awards or objects, such as coins, flat seashells, collectible cards, and pieces of cloth, yarn, or thread. You can even store audio cassette

BEANIE BABIES. Artist: Staci Nash.
Using border, animal, letter stickers, and journaling with a pen, a fad of the times is collected into mem-ories of childhood. Make a border with stickers and adhere letters for the title. Mount the cropped pho-tos and decorate with additional stickers.

△ ICE HOCKEY. (background) Artist: Becki Burgeron.
ICE SKATING. (foreground) Artist: Tawnya Parker.
Each of these sports pages is accented by a staple aspect
of the sport. The hockey stick boasts Chris's number for
the season; the "ice skating" letters are sleek and
descriptive, like ice sculptures.

▷ FISHING. Artist: Cindy Bess.
What a great way to pass on treasured family tradi-
tions.Use colored and printed paper, fancy scissors,
stickers, and die cuts and pens. Crop and mat the photos, then mount the die cuts and stickers. For the title,
layer dark-colored letters behind light-colored letters.

tapes of musical recitals. Remember to protect photographs from contact with memorabilia with
PVC-safe page protectors.

Be creative when decorating your album pages. Find ways to include objects and symbols asso-
ciated with the activity. For example, crop the photos of your hockey player into shapes and position him flying across the ice. Crop out the piano bench beneath your little musician and sit her on
a hand-drawn treble clef. Cut mats into balls, banjos, bells, or other objects related to the hobby.
Look for stickers, stamps, and papers decorated with images related to the collection or activity.

Fishing

My First Catch

Papa's boat was named for me "Cindy Lee"

SCHOOL ALBUMS

~~~

School days, good-old golden rule days. They were filled with reading, writing, and "rithmetic," but also with friendship, team work, and self-reliance. We spent most of our growing-up years within those walls laden with crayoned art work and chalk-scrawled blackboards. And the sights, smells, and sounds of the schoolroom are just as familiar to our children.

Whether you are making an album of your school years or of your child's, you will want to fill the pages with class photos, individual portraits, and snapshots of school activites. Be sure to also include photos of classmates and notes written by them or to them.

Personalize the album with report cards, progress reports, awards, book reports, math assignments—and those elaborate maps for geography class on which you (or your child) painstakingly hand-labeled all fifty state capitals!

Look for colors and decorative elements that support the theme. School colors might be a good choice—also, punched books, apples, pencils, and see-saws. You can buy or make templates for letters and numbers. Arrange colorful stickers into a schoolroom border. With some easy paper

cutting and a little tape or glue, you can set a photo of a child's shiny face right in the middle of an apple-shaped mat.

If you or your parents didn't keep your old notebooks and homework assignments, contact your school you attended. It may have old photographs and a copy of your records on file. Ask to borrow and copy photos from former classmates. Ask them to share some of their written memories with you, too. Check the local library for copies of articles about your alma mater. If you were an athlete or won academic awards, you might even be mentioned in print!

△ *PRETTY PRAIRIE GRADUATES.*
Artist: Susan Sigle.
Documenting high school heritage (mother, father, and daughter all graduated from the same high school) can be a great way to tie family pictures together.

◁ *FIRST DAY OF KINDERGARTEN.*
Artist: Lisa Dixon.
Adapting a sampler pattern to fit your particular photo is as easy as stitching a design on perforated paper, cutting out the patch, and mounting it on colored paper along with cropped photos.

◁◁ *THE MAGIC SCHOOL BUS.*
Artist: Anne Thompson.
Get creative with those school photos! Freehand-cut the bus, or make a pattern by copying and enlarging the one shown here. Cut bus wheels using circle templates, and freehand-cut headlights and bumpers. Cut out windows with a craft knife, or mount white rectangles instead. Draw other bus parts with a black pen.

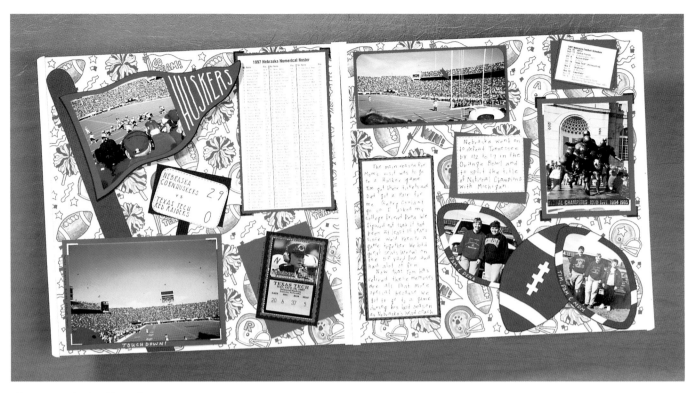

HUSKERS. Artist: Pam Joutras.
Requiring only colored and printed paper, fancy scissors, and pens, this fun page is alive with football spirit. The football paper works perfectly in the background and the freehand-cut flag and footballs are ideal mats for photos. Added memorabilia will complete the spirited feeling.

Whether you plan to begin a school album for your child now or sometime in the future, here are some tips for building a library of great materials.

❖ Volunteer to be the class photographer. Attend events and parties with camera in hand and capture the moments as they unfold. Make extra copies for display in the classroom or for a teacher album, a wonderful end-of-the-year class gift for a beloved instructor.

❖ Start a file or find a box to hold your child's schoolwork. Save the average efforts as well as the exceptional. Be sure to date each paper and report to make it easier to organize them in the future.

❖ Encourage your child to keep a school journal. The stories and events he or she writes about now will make wonderful album pages later.

❖ Keep a journal of your own. Write about your child's growth and changing attitudes about school. Jot down the names of friends, the titles of favorite books, and funny things said or done that relate to school days. Record your own feelings as your child masters new skills and concepts.

Create an album for each year of a child's education, or group elementary school photos and secondary school photos into separate books. And don't forget those high school and college years! The learning never stops—and neither do the possibilities for creating school albums.

FRIENDSHIP ALBUMS

~~

She helped you up when you skinned your knee in first grade. She held your hand when the first boy to hold your heart tossed it to the wind. She was by your side when a better man vowed to keep you safe forever. She held your infant that first day home from the hospital, the joy in her face mirroring your own. She's your best friend.

A friendship album honors those special friends who have filled your life with meaning and laughter. You can structure the book so that it moves from the past to the present, dedicate pages to individual friends, or design pages around events ("First Grade Memories" or "A Grand Graduation").

You probably already have boxes filled with me-and-my-friend photographs—but if you don't, start taking them now. Set up photo shoots with friends from the past and the present. While you're clicking away, you're sure to be rekindling memories that will make great journaled passages in your album. (Send each friend a photocopy of the page on which she appears as a thank-you for her help and friendship.)

△ *GOOD BUDDIES—MADELINE AND ANDREW WILBUR. Photographer: Eric Wilbur.*

▷ *SASHA. Artist: Michele Gerbrandt.*
Have you ever wondered what to do with all those portraits of your child? Surprise your friends with a thoughtful gift of a striking scrapbook page.

GIFT ALBUMS

❖❖❖

Whether made for a beloved grandparent, teacher, coach, or friend, gift albums—like friendship albums—are made with someone special in mind. A gift album doesn't have to be completed all at once. You may wish to give the album to the recipient with only a handful of pages within the book. Then, as you collect more photos over time, simply create more pages. Wrap the additional pages and give them as gifts for Mother's Day, Father's Day, holidays, and birthdays. The recipient will eagerly anticipate receiving each new page.

Albums are wonderful end-of-the-year gifts for classes or teams to give to their favorite teachers, youth ministers, or coaches. They are even more special when children contribute to them. Title some blank sheets of photo-safe paper—for example, "I'll Always Remember," "Times You Made Me Laugh," "You Taught Me." Hand out the sheets to the class or team and ask the children to write letters to the album's recipient addressing those topics. Encourage them to illustrate their letters, too. Ask other parents for photographs and ask the children to photocopy any awards they received while in the teacher's class or on the coach's team. Ask them to include copies of schoolwork they are proud of, including poems and stories. When you've collected all the materials, either design and compile the album yourself or invite small groups of children to work on the pages with you.

TRIBUTE TO GRANDFATHER. Artist: Katie Kight. This gift album was made as a Christmas gift from grandchildren and great-grandchildren for a special Grandpa. This well-thought-out book starts with a recent photo of Grandpa and a poem written for him. Each two-page layout following was based on a line of the poem.

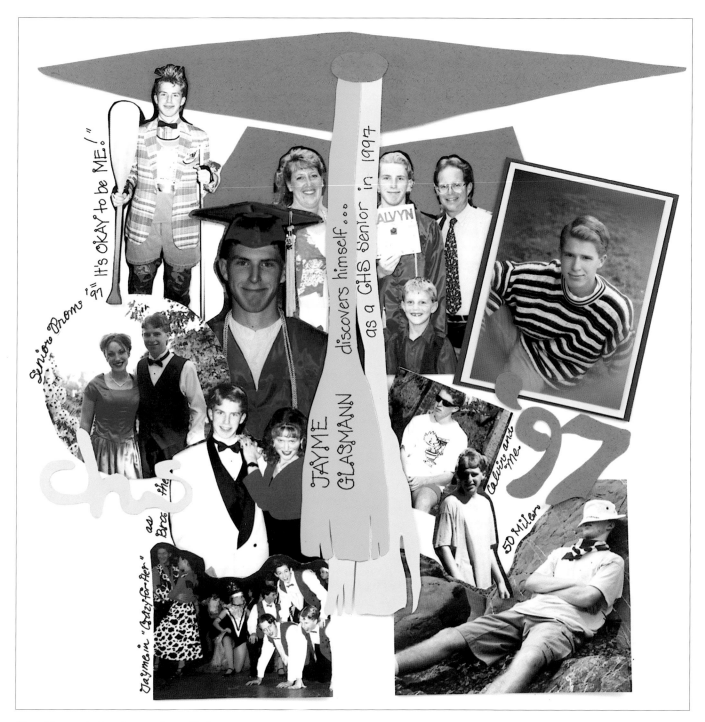

Senior Prom '97 "It's OKAY to be ME."

Seniors Prom "Crazy to Her"

chs

discovers himself...
as a CHS Senior in 1997

JAYME GLASMANN

Calvin and me

50 Milers

'97

Boy Teen. Artist: Lorna Dee Christensen.
Remembering your teen's experiences on scrapbook pages can be a rewarding project, one that you can approach in several ways. You can create a personal album with social and academic highlights or you might focus on a favorite activity that defines your child's focus. Take the time to find the best photos possible and then crop, mat, and mount them. This lively page uses a mortar board as the central image. Cropped and captioned photos are all that are needed to complete the picture. A commemorative album is a generous gift that can be especially poignant when given at a rite of passage like graduation.

JASON & GIGI

McMichael's Prom
Stoneville
April 1997

Before you wrap and present a finished gift album, photocopy the pages. Those who helped create the volume may want to include pages in their own life, school, or hobby scrapbooks. You'll want a copy for your own library, too, as a reminder of the special person who made the effort worthwhile.

JASON AND GIGI. Artist: Joyce Schweitzer. The heart page provides a romantic backdrop for a portrait taken just before an evening at a high school prom. A simple palette, a heart template, special scissors, and a few small heart stickers are all you need.

FRIENDLY ADDITIONS

Fill your friendship-album pages with stickers, stamps, and punches that say "you're special to me." Here are just a few ideas:

❖ STICKERS: *Large and small hearts, flowers, children playing, XOXO (hugs and kisses), dancing or hugging animals, stars*

❖ STAMPS: *Superstar, happy face, tea cup, kiss print, hearts, hugging teddy, friendly pets, "Friends Forever" and other sentiments*

❖ PUNCHES: *Angel, heart, lamb, telephone, flower, lovebirds, happy face, starburst*

ABC ALBUMS

A is for Amelia, the star of the book! Her grandmother has put together a special album to help her learn to read. ABC albums are wonderful tools to help preschoolers learn the alphabet. Each page features photos, stickers, die cuts, and memorabilia that represent people, places, objects, actions, or emotions related to a letter. For example, on the A page, there may be a photo of a child eating an apple, an airplane sticker, an alligator die cut, and a few hand-lettered words that begin with the letter A.

To get started, organize photos, memorabilia, and decorative elements into piles of different categories, arranged alphabetically:

OBJECTS (apple, bear, cat . . .)   *ACTIONS* (growl, hit, itch . . .)

NAMES (Mary, Nathan, Olive . . .)   *EMOTIONS* (sad, tired, unhappy . . .)

SOUNDS (waaah, xxxx, yikes, zzzz)

Many of your photos will fit into more than one category, but base your decision on the primary images. If some of your letter pages don't have many photographs, fill the pages with die cuts, stickers, or punch designs—or simply take a new photograph to represent that letter.

Some scrapbookers modify and expand their ABC albums to teach the months of the year, days of the week, numbers, and simple shapes. These concepts can be incorporated into the alphabet pages or can have pages of their own.

ABC ALBUMS. Artists: (Top) Vanessa Murphy. (Bottom) Carole Hadovec-Farley.
An alphabetical format works for just about any album theme, from pages that are just for fun to more specific personal record-keeping. Alphabet pages can also be excellent educational tools for children learning their ABC's and 123's.

TRIBUTE OR MEMORIAL ALBUMS

Whether you live in a small town or a booming metropolis, you are sure to know a special person who gives more than she or he receives, who is quick to laugh and first to help. Honor this remarkable person with a tribute album. Or create a memorial album for a special person who is deceased. Tribute albums make wonderful gifts, and memorial albums are a comfort to grieving family members. Both are inspired by the spirits of those whose pictures adorn the pages.

The biggest challenge will be collecting and organizing the material. To document a person's lifetime, you'll need to work with many years' worth of materials. Early photographs and stories may be hard to find. Begin by locating people who knew the subject of your album during his or her childhood or early adulthood. Ask relatives or friends, or consult class lists or school yearbooks. Send postcards to those who might help, asking for some written information about themselves and the ways the person influenced their lives and memorable times they shared.

If the person you are honoring is a member of your family, hold a family reunion. Set album pages on the tables and ask guests to take a few minutes to write in them. Ask to borrow photos from everyone you contact and make duplicates.

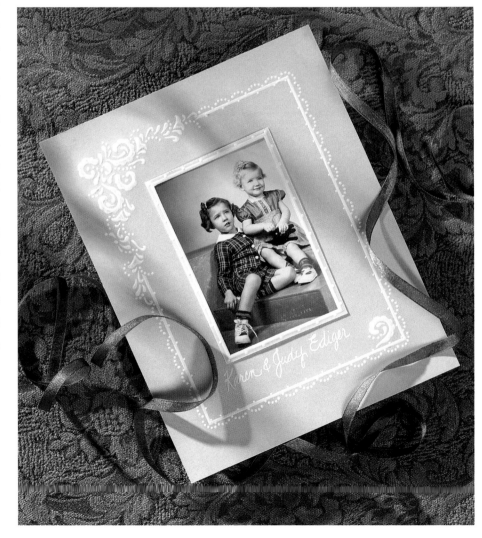

KAREN AND JUDY. Artist: Pam Klassen.
A single template and vellum paper were used to create the elegant white embossed frame supporting an exquisite heirloom photo. Brown paper mounted behind the vellum tints it with soft color. The understated frame is all that is needed to complete the nostalgic page.

Most albums begin with old photographs, so consider starting with a "period" look, incorporating the colors and fabrics of that time period in the decorative details. Update the look and feel of the book as it moves forward in time—for example, an album's elegant, formal first pages might become poodle-skirt pink in the 1950s and embellished with wild neon colors in the 1960s.

Add photocopies of sheet music, movie posters, and book covers that were popular during decades of the subject's life. If you have permission, also include copies of diary entries and letters written by the person.

HERITAGE ALBUMS

T he year was 1944, and although they'd been married for more than a decade, the love they shared was still evident in the way she tipped her head to look at his face and the way his arm circled her waist. A camera caught the moment and held it so that generations to come could share in their grandparent's pleasure.

Old photos are a treasure. A heritage album displays these precious old photographs to honor those at the root of our family tree and to celebrate who we are. It makes a wonderful "coffee-table" book and conversation piece. You'll often find yourself and your family poring over its pages, telling "I remember when" stories to the next generation of scrapbookers.

LILLIAN HILL. Artist: Joyce Schweitzer.
A stunning heritage album page preserves the fresh face of a lovely young woman photographed more than fifty years ago. The mauve and purple palette as well as the wavy-edged oval-shaped photograph are appropriate reminders of the romance and glamour of bygone days.

A heritage album begins with research. Look for information in genealogical charts and family trees, old letters and diaries, newspaper clippings, and birth, marriage, and death certificates. But the greatest wealth of materials will probably come from older family members. Earliest memories are the last to fade, and, with a little encouragement, the elderly enjoy telling their detailed stories of years long gone to an appreciative audience.

Organizing old photographs can be a big job. Begin by sorting them into piles based on either time period or family lineage. Don't feel that you need to use every photo you have. Select only those that tell the story best and work well together—save the rest for future books.

Number or code each photo on the back with a graphite pencil or with a sticky note. On a separate sheet, write the names of the people in the photographs and any details about the event, place, or time. Store each pile of photos in a photo-safe envelope until you are ready to use them.

In general, avoid cropping historical photos. What appears in the background often helps to tell the story, providing colorful details about the place and the period. Cropping may eliminate valuable information.

A heritage album is a specific theme project, which means you can plan the entire book before beginning to assemble it. Heritage albums are suited to a chronological format (from most distant past to most recent), but can also be organized by the various branches of the family tree.

Some scrapbookers select a color to represent each branch of the family. Use album pages, mats, and die cuts of the same color on all the pages for those family members. Variations on the color can be used to identify each generation. For example, if you've chosen red for one family branch, you might use red checks or red flowers to show the generations of children and grandchildren. If a member from the red branch of the family married a member from the blue branch, you might mat their children's pictures with purple.

CARING FOR HISTORICAL PHOTOS

Old, fragile photographs need to be handled with extreme care. Use only acid-free, lignin-free papers and safe adhesives and ink in your album. Non-permanent mounting techniques, such as photo corners and plastic sleeves, will allow you to remove the photo at a later time in order to have it restored or copied.

THE ALLYN FAMILY. *Artist: Laurie Capener.*
Family portraits are presented, one image per page, in an elegant Victorian style using decoratively cut and layered mats for the portraits and nameplates. The soft colors are warm and inviting. Subtle color is well-suited to these heirloom photos.

FAMILY TREES

B ranch out from that traditional stick-and-line drawing. Try drawing an oak tree on the album page, letting its broad limbs represent families of ancestors. Or draw an apple tree and place photos of family members inside shiny, red apples. You don't have to go out on a limb to have fun with your family tree!

LIFE ALBUMS

❧

When all is said and done, the day-to-day events are what we will remember best—the springtime walks around the block, a child's first smile after the braces come off, the first afternoon your kindergartner spent with a new puppy. A life album is an ongoing record of these special moments.

Life albums are actually multiple-theme albums. They combine photos of holidays and celebrations, weddings, vacations, sports activities, and hobbies all in one book. Life albums are ongoing projects that evolve and grow as time passes, new photos are taken, and more pages are added, so they are usually structured chronologically.

To avoid pages with a haphazard look, take some time to think about the album's style and look before beginning to assemble it. One of the best ways to create a harmonious effect is to decide on some key words that describe your album: for example, "bright, simple, childlike, and whimsical" or "elegant, romantic, and old-fashioned." Jot the words down on a piece of paper and keep it as a reminder of the effect you wish to achieve as you create pages.

Another helpful way to ensure consistency is to select a color palette for your album. Choose colors that suit your album's style and carry them throughout the book.

Those who don't want the book to have a single style can create multiple-page sections within the book. Two- or four-page photo spreads might be grouped around an event or theme—for instance, a holiday or special vacation. Or consider adding timelines or year-in-review pages, too.

Journaling within life albums can help put the photos in a larger context of place, time, and significance. You can use bullets and captions, but be sure to include some funny and special stories, too.

A life album is a wonderful project for busy scrapbookers because it can be put together a little bit at a time, rather than in one long, demanding period. If there's simply too much going on in your life to begin or continue working on a life album, don't worry. Set the photos and memorabilia aside. Over time, you'll gain some perspective, and it will be easier to weed out photographs and organize the pages.

◁ *FAMILY TREE. Artist: Marsha Schuppe.*
A walk in the park turned into a delightful family tree-climbing adventure. One photo is silhouetted to form the tree trunk and the rest of the photos (7) are cropped and cut into circles and matted with green paper cut with decorative scissors.

▷ *(overleaf) TIME LINE. Artist: Anita Hickinbotham.*
Any graduate would be thrilled to receive this gift. Cropped photos, black pens, stickers, and your own thoughtfulness are all you need to create this stunning album page. Stickers and cropped photos document the events and activities.

IT'S A GIRL!

February 26, 1979

first love "Oatmeal!"

one year old!

childhood toys

Tyler born

1980

1981

travel!

youth camp

Smoky

we Moo-ve to the country

YMCA Youth Choir

GFC youth camp

winter play

1989

1988

sunning with friends

GFC Youth Camp

Autumn Days

Home School Again!

1990

"Costuming" with friends

Rehoboth Beach with Larry and Marcia

Lia born

always writing letters!?

Quarter master at Youth Camp

First place - Buckeye regionals

BEST

Volunteer days at Ohio Village

Sewing period dress with

1994

Acquire the Fire!

Mission Trip to Japan

Working at Burger King

Bake Sales for Mission Trip

Mexico with Teen Mania

Cade born

driver's license

Youth Camp Counselor

Youth Camp Jr. Counselor

1995

1996

SOURCES

~~~

Page 2
Daisy Border: Erica Pierovich

Page 3
Photos by: Charlene Tritt

Page 5
ABIGAIL: Pam Klassen
    Lasting Impressions
    (801) 298-1979
    585 W. 2600 So. #A
    Bountiful, UT 84010

Page 8
MOTHER'S LOVE: Vine Die Cut
    Ellison Craft & Design
    (800) 253-2238
    25862 Commercentre Dr.
    Lake Forest, CA 92630-8804

Page 17:
Photobox:
    Exposures
    (800) 222-4947
Memorabilia box:
    Light Impressions
    (800) 828-6216

Page 19
Mug:
    © Remember It Well
    (888) 639-6393
    5636 Orchard Way
    W. Palm Beach, FL 33417

Page 20
Photo: Joyce Feil

Page 25
Strap-Style Albums:
    Creative Memories
    (800) 468-9335
    P.O. Box 1839
    St. Cloud, MN 56302-1839
Post-Bound Albums:
    Artistic Memories
    (800) 888-6004
    1945 N. Fairfield
    Chicago, IL 60647
Binder Albums:
    Hiller Industries
    (801) 521-2411
    631 North 400 West
    Salt Lake City, UT 84103
Spiral-Bound Albums:
    Canson-Talens, Inc.
    (800) 628-9283
    21 Industrial Dr., P.O. Box 220
    So. Hadley, MA 01075

Page 29
Photos on page by: Joyce Feil

Page 31
FLOWER GIRL: Stamps
Double Heart L153, Patch Heart B164, Bold
Square C124, Flower Border E123, and Creative
Frame Set CFC811:
    Northern Spy
    (916) 620-7430
    P.O. Box 2735
    Placerville, CA 95667

Page 32
JIMMY AND GIGI:
Penguin stickers #SP-FZ-02:
    Stickopotamus
    (800) 524-1349
    P.O. Box 86
    Carlstadt, NJ 07072-0086

Page 33
TRUE LOVE: Heart Stickers
    Mrs. Grossman's Paper Co.
    (800) 457-4570
    3810 Cypress Dr.
    Petaluma, CA 94954-5613

Page 34
HOPSCOTCH: Geometric stickers:
    Mrs. Grossman's Paper Co.
    See listing for page 33

Page 35
Snowflake stamps:
    The Happy Stamper
    (303) 322-2489
    2703 E. 3rd Ave.
    Denver, CO 80206

Page 36
SABRINA: photos used with permission
    of Lisa Hegro, Los Angeles, CA
Stickers:
    Mrs. Grossman's Paper Co.
    See listing for page 33

Pages 42–43
TIPTOE THROUGH THE TULIPS: Tulip
    die cut:
    Ellison Craft & Design
    See listing for page 8

Page 44:
YOU ARE MY SUNSHINE:
    Ellison Craft & Design
    See listing for page 8

Page 45
4TH OF JULY: Flag stickers:
    Francis Meyer, Inc.
    (800) 372-6237
    P.O. Box 3088
    Savannah, GA 31402
    (wholesale only)
Star Stickers:
    Mrs. Grossman's Paper Co.
    See listing for page 33

Page 46
Templates:
    Family Treasures
    (800) 413-2645
    24992 Anza Ave. Unit A
    Valencia, CA 91355

Pages 48-49
GOING FOR A DIP: Die cuts
    Ellison Craft & Design
    See listing for page 8
Fish Punch:
    Westrim Crafts®/Memories
    Forever™
    (818) 998-8550
    9667 Canoga Ave.
    Chatsworth, CA 91311

Page 50
Papers:
The Paper Patch
    (800) 397-2737
    P.O. Box 414
    Riverton, UT 84065

Page 51
AMY GILBERT:
    Papercuttings by Alison
    (914) 957-0328
    P.O. Box 2771
    Sarasota, FLA 34230
    Photo: Joyce Feil

Page 55
CAMPING IN THE MOONLIGHT:
Moon and tree die cuts:
    Ellison Craft & Design
    See listing for page 8

Page 59
SUNBEAMS: "Sunbeams" poem:
Harris, M.A., *Baby's First Book of
    Angels*, © 1995
    Brownlow Publishing Co.,
    Ft. Worth, TX.
Cloud wrapping paper: Papier

Page 60
FOURTH OF JULY: Firecracker die cuts:
    Creative Memories
    See listing for page 25

Page 61
MAKE A JOYFUL NOISE:
Staff notes cut free hand from own
template
Note stickers:
    Mrs. Grossman's Paper Co.
    See listing for page 33
Letter Stickers:
    Making Memories
    (800) 286-5263
    P.O. Box 1188
    Centerville, UT 84014

Page 65
NEW MEXICO:
    Core Composition
    Apple of Your Eye
    Salt Lake City, UT

Page 69
A ROSE BY ANY OTHER NAME:
Flower stickers:
    The Gifted Line
    (800) 5-GIFTED
    999 Canal Blvd.
    Point Richmond, CA 94804
Printed paper:
    Hot Off The Press
    (503) 266-9102
    1250 NW Third
    Canby, OR 97013

Page 73
PUMPKIN MONTAGE:
Scarecrow and leaf rubber stamps:
    Close to My Hearts/D.O.T.S.
    (888) 655-6552
    738 E. Quality Dr.
    American Forks, UT 84003